THE HAPPY SIDE
OF LIFE

By: Gina Greene

PublishAmerica
Baltimore

First printing

Hardcover 978-1-4626-1178-2
Softcover 978-1-4626-1179-9
PUBLISHED BY PUBLISHAMERICA, LLLP
www.publishamerica.com
Baltimore

Printed in the United States of America

I thank God continually for my "Prince Charming", husband, O.J....
It is to him that I lovingly dedicate this book.

Psalm 30:11 Thou hast turned for me

My mourning into dancing: thou hast put

Off my sackcloth, and girded me with

Gladness;

ACKNOWLEDGEMENTS

No one knows better than I do that I am not a writer. But I want to thank all the people whom God used to encourage me and to physically help me in this long endeavor.

First of all, thank you, O.J. Without your loving reassurances I would have stopped long before the book was finished. It was your willingness and even insistence that enabled me to tell our story undisguised.

To Tiffany, Trey and Jeni, thank you for your confidence that "Mom" would one day complete the story YOU knew God had given me. Please forgive me for all the times I didn't have time.

Thank you to our Parents. You are to be commended for not fainting as you discovered the frank and shocking truths of those earlier years.

Then to my sister, Elaine, I want to say thank you for your honest correction of my miserable grammar and spelling. We had such fun reading over my many comical mistakes.

Without you, Marion West, to guide me by your positive attitudes and clear directions on my manuscript, none of this would be possible. Thank you.

Jim Reimann, you were the first person to make me believe it was possible for me to write a book and perhaps even have it published. Thank you for sharing my dream.

Thank you, Bob Hill, for your honest criticism and positive encouragement to never give up until my goal was at last completed.

Jane Fields, Lynn Long and Glenda Tolbert, you were my back-ups. When I said, "I can't do it"! you always cheered me on. To you and all the other dear friends who loved me through it all, thank you!

Finally, a very special thanks to you Donna Mackay. Only an extraordinary person would volunteer to type my final manuscript.

Thank you, Lord for gently leading me through the many painful lessons in my life and for allowing me to share them with all these wonderful people.

I love you all dearly!

SITTING BY MY LAUGHING FIRE

I met you years ago

When

Of all the men

I knew,

You, I hero-worshipped then:

You are my husband now…

My husband!

And from my home

(your arms)

I turn to look

Down the long trail of years

To where I met you first

And hero-worshipped,

And I would smile'

…I know you better now:

The faults,

The odd preferments,

The differences

That make you, YOU.

That other me,

- So young

- So far away-

- Saw you

- And hero-worshipped

But never KNEW:

While I

Grown wiser

With the closeness of these years,

Hero-worship, too!

By Ruth Bell Graham

WORLD BOOKS PUBLISHER

Contents

CHAPTER I
THE LONG DARK NIGHT

Psalm 30:5…."Weeping may endure for a night, but joy cometh in the morning."

We were flying along at 35,000 ft. above the ocean, but I felt that I was sinking into a bottomless pit. It was to be our second honeymoon, this "exciting" trip to Jamaica! However, as we sat there, strangers, each of us wearing our beautiful disguises, I knew something was about to happen. I don't think I was prepared for what did happen!

Suddenly, almost like a slap that jarred me back into reality, I heard this stranger, my husband, saying "Why don't we have just one glass of champagne to celebrate?" The flight attendant stood smiling, waiting for an answer, but honestly I could not say a word. I kept thinking, "I thought that was all over, a thing of the past! What am I doing here anyway? I can't! I just cannot!" It was like going back 5 years. All the pain, the heartache of alcohol, mingled with hate flooded my memory.

After we landed, things didn't get any better. I had hoped so desperately that this would be a time of really getting to know one another.

Oh sure, we had been married ten years. I knew how he liked his eggs, no sugar in his coffee, and just what to say to send him off in a temper fit. But, I mean the real person – the inside of his heart was what I longed to see and understand.

We tried walks on the beach in the moonlight, and rides in the countryside. We rented a Volkswagen that had the steering wheel on the right side. (That was the "brightest" part of the whole trip.) We had thought getting away from everyone else would bring us closer together. It was impossible, however, to find anything to talk about. Being alone was painfully awkward for us. Everything seemed empty, and finally we both admitted we wanted to go home. We made some flimsy excuse about missing the children and left a day early.

The last night of our trip, we took one last walk on the beach, hoping to discover some common ground between us. Years of hurt and bitterness had worn away all the dreams and hopes we had once shared. We agreed the only approach to our seemingly hopeless situation was total honesty. We were able to agree on one thing, our marriage was going NOWHERE!

"I DON'T THINK I LOVE YOU ANY LONGER", MY HUSBAND ADMITTED!

My first thoughts were to run into the ocean and never look back. I screamed and begged God to tell me what I could do! At last, I realized, there was nothing "I" could do!

Three months prior to this I had made a complete commitment of my will to the Lord. I kept saying, "Lord, I promised to serve you no matter, what but I didn't know this would be the WHAT! I kept searching desperately for an answer to all the chaos taking place in my own heart, when God in His sweet, faithful way led me to a book I had on my own book shelf. Some dear friends had given us Keith Miller's book, THE TASTE OF NEW WINE, a few years earlier and I had never bothered to read it. In it Keith tells of his inward struggle and final surrender. I felt I was totally able to identify with him. At that time, I realized that for ten long years I had prayed for God to save my husband and then we BOTH would serve Him. In the meanwhile, I did nothing! I never considered that serving Christ was a walk one must choose regardless of anyone else's position. It was then that I decided for the first time to take my stand for Christ no matter what the cost.

I told the Lord that I would serve Him WITH or WITHOUT my husband. I would serve Him even if it meant divorce or death. Job 13:15, "Though He slay me, yet will I trust in Him…" I had no idea at that time just what this decision would involve.

I claimed some promises in the Bible that I knew I could hold onto. I Peter 3: 1&2 "likewise ye wives be in subjection to your own husbands, that if any obey not the Word, they also may without the Word be won by the conversation of the wives; while they behold your chaste conversation coupled with fear," and Galatians 6:9, " And let us not be weary in well doing; for in due season we shall reap, if we faint not."

I cannot say that I was always a great success in my new decision, but I can say that Christ was always there to lift me up and encourage me to try, try again. During those long months, I must have asked the Lord "WHY" one million and ten times. I believe now I know what was happening. My marriage was like a giant boil that had been festering for ten painful years. God had to bring all the poison to the surface, so that He could finally lance and heal the pain.

II Corinthians 4:17, " For our light affliction, which is but for a moment worketh for us a far more exceeding and eternal weight of glory:"

CHAPTER II
'ON MY FEET', I SAID

Proverbs 8:17..."Those that seek me early shall find me."

My earliest recollections of God were in an old unpainted country church at the age of five. We only had services twice a month because the pastor was a circuit preacher with others churches in nearby towns. There was only a handful of faithful members which got to be to an even smaller group in the summer. The only air conditioning was open windows and hand fans made of cardboard on a stick. There were two revivals each year, and everybody from all around would walk to the evening services.

I can remember hearing the preacher and deacons pray and thinking, "It must be wonderful to know for sure that you're going to Heaven when you die. Of course, I also thought that no one but a preacher or real "worker" in the church could know for sure, so I never bothered to ask anyone about it. I did continue to go to church and became very faithful in my attendance as I approached my teens. It was the popular thing to do; go to church and later stay for the youth fellowship where there was always "bunches" of cute boys.

When I was 12 years old my family moved from the country to Mobile, Alabama. The big city was exciting for me and every day was a new adventure.

Mother told me that my choice of religion would be up to me because she felt it was a very personal thing. I can only thank God that He was so faithful to keep His hand on me in those early years. The nagging thought of Hell began to enter my mind about this time and I started my search for an answer.

One day I happened upon a lovely plaque that had the "Ten Commandments" beautifully embellished in gold and this seemed the perfect solution for me. Each night as I would say my "Lay me down to sleep prayers," I would go down the List of commandments, hoping desperately that I had managed to keep all of the commandments. Of course, I wasn't sure what all of them meant, but I just figured if I could not understand it, I couldn't possibly DO it!

Then, one beautiful, glorious day I met a young man named Mel, who asked me to attend church with him. This was one of my first real dates and I was very impressed. I also found myself strangely drawn to his church. It was very different from my church. I say "my church" because I had joined the church with the appealing youth activities. I was at the magic age of 13 and needed desperately to "belong," just to be a part of something.

I remember the day I finally got up the nerve to walk down the aisle to join this church (social club.) I was wearing my first pair of high heels, blue ones, and my legs wobbled all the way down the long aisle.

Upon arriving at the front, I was met by the Pastor who asked me how I came. "On my feet", I said! I had no idea at all what he was talking about. I had made up my mind earlier that morning to join the church because of rebellion to something Mother had said. I had been telling her about the activities at "My Church", when she declared that it was not "My Church", since I was not a member. I decided right then and there. "I'll show Her! I'll make it "My Church"- and I did!

The Pastor said, "I mean, do you want to be baptized?" At which time I answered, "If that's what you have to do to become a member of this church, then I want to be baptized. And baptized I was – knowing absolutely nothing at all about the meaning of baptism or salvation –just pure and simple REBELLION.

This was all I knew of church or salvation until Mel introduced me to his church and finally to his Savior. One day as we were walking to church he asked me if I was a Christian and if I knew just how to get to Heaven.

"Of course, I do", was my reply, meaning the keeping of the law and doing the very best you knew how to do. However, Mel must have sensed that I had no idea at all of how to gain Heaven and miss Hell so he proceeded to tell me anyway. Mel said, "You know going to Heaven doesn't depend on anything WE do. Jesus did it all for us on Calvary and all we must do is trust Him." He went on to explain how we must be "born again" and accept Christ by faith. He read John Chapter 3 to me about the religious man named Nicodemus who came to Jesus asking Him, "How does one go about inheriting eternal life"?

John 3:16 took on a different meaning to me as I read the words, "For God so loved the world (Gina) that He gave His only begotten Son, that whosoever (Gina) believeth in Him shall not perish, but have everlasting life." I would not pray and trust Christ with Mel that day because of my awful pride, but later in my own room, I lay in bed and wept as I poured out a lifetime of searching and despair.

I trusted Christ as my personal Savior that night and found a new beginning along with an end to the bondage of trying to keep the law. Oh, I didn't hear any bells or see any flashing lights, but I knew Christ had come into my life, and I had a new peace that I had never felt before.

This began a busy, happy, exciting time for me. Bob Harrington, The Chaplain of Bourbon Street was in Mobile and had just gotten saved that same year. I was 15, and life held so many promises. Bob was holding tent revivals, and traveling around in an old truck that he called "The Gospel Wagon." A group of us kids from "Youth for Christ" would follow him around and hand out tracts while he preached. I remember one day was particularly exciting. We stopped at a local bar and passed the tracts out to the people as they would come out. I had the feeling of being involved in some dangerous mission for my Lord, and I loved it!

CHAPTER III
SEND WHO?

Isaiah 6:8 "Also I heard the voice of the Lord, saying, "Whom shall I send and who will go for us?" Then said I. Here am I; send me."

Mother and Daddy thought I had lost my mind. They both had been raised in very conservative homes and felt religion was a very quiet and personal matter. They had "endured" all the stages with me that most young girls fall prey to, but this was something for which they were totally unprepared. Suddenly, their moody self-centered daughter began to sail around 90 miles an hour finding things to do for her new Lord. I must admit, however, I must have looked a little crazy to just about everybody, including the Lord. I was busy hanging up posters, saying, "Repent, for the Kingdom of Heaven is at hand", and slipping tracts in the mailbox at the Jewish Shrine! Finally I landed on an idea at school to start a "Youth for Christ" Club. We would meet once a week in an old boy scout building, that should have been condemned.

It had an old wood stove that we used for a heater and a few boxes that served as chairs. In between jumping up and down to testify, we always had someone share how Christ could transform our lives. We really did manage to get some terrific speakers, the main one being

Bob Harrington, and many kids came to know Christ as a result of all the belue.

Mel had gone away to Bible School to study to be a preacher. On one of his holidays at home he asked me to be his wife. I quickly accepted and began immediately to plan to become a preacher's wife. (The best laid plans of mice and men.) Then, one night a strange thing happened to me. God began to deal with my heart in a very new and different way about the Mission Field. It was a thought that consumed me completely and I simply could not shake it. I opened my Bible to Isaiah 6:8 and read the words over and over again, until at last I surrendered and asked the Lord to PLEASE SEND ME!

I felt very sure that God had called me to go to the Holy Land, the very place from which He had left, to carry His Word. I longed and ached to go. I had heard many people say that God had called them to a particular place or purpose, but always wondered until that night just how it happened.

There are really no words to describe the dealings of God with a person, but as the Prophet said in I Kings 19:11-12 "And, behold the Lord passed by and a great and strong wind rent the mountains and brake in pieces the rocks before the Lord; but the Lord was not in the wind; and after the wind the earthquake; but the Lord was not in the earthquake; and after the earthquake a fire; but the Lord was not in the fire; and after the fire a still small voice." It's that "still small voice" that I learned to listen to as it whispers so gently to my heart.

The next morning I could hardly wait to tell everyone – except Mel. How could I tell him that I could not marry him, because God had called me to go to the Mission Field? But, the phone rang before I was even out of bed and guess who! Yep – Mel! I could hardly believe my ears as he poured out his heart to me. He was talking so fast and excited that I had a hard time understanding him, but at last I heard the words. "I've known for some time that God wanted me to preach the Gospel, but last night God showed me a particular place where He wanted me to carry His message. And guess where! The Holy Land!"

I know most people would say it was just a coincidence, or that it was just crazy young people, but I believe that it was the directing hand of Almighty God. The next step was to tell my parents. I knew they were not going to be over joyed at the prospect, but I had completely underestimated their reactions. Mother almost fainted and Daddy yelled! Finally, the preacher was called in and he assured them that we would not be leaving for the Mission Field tomorrow or for that matter, any time soon. There must be years of school and preparation. I could not possibly know at that time that I would never realize this calling and dream. My rebellion and self will would lead me off in another direction that would cost me many tragic years before finding new direction from the Lord.

CHAPTER IV
THANK YOU LORD

Luke 19:9 "This day is Salvation come to this House."

My parents built a new house and we moved out into the suburbs. This was the culmination of a lifelong dream for Mother and Daddy. They had worked hard all their life and always wanted to own their own home. It was a fresh new brick ranch situated on a lovely acre with tall pines and beautiful blooming azaleas.

It was here that we found a new church, which we all began attending together for the first time. There was so much conflict in my heart. I wanted to serve the Lord, but I just found it so hard to be submissive to my parents. I felt that since they were not Christians I did not have to obey them.

In fact, I counted it blessings from the Lord when they were upset with me. I would quote the verses in Luke 12:51, "Suppose ye that I am come to give peace on earth? I tell you, Nay, but rather division: For from henceforth there shall be five in one house divided, three against two, and two against three. The father shall be divided against the son, and the son against the father; the mother against the daughter and the daughter against the mother."

Now I know that I was so very wrong. God never intended children to use those verses for excuses to rebel against their parents. Actually, it was not until I had children of my own that I learned God's precious chain of command. I wish someone had told me about Galatians 3:20 "Children, obey your parents in All Things, for this is well pleasing unto the Lord."

It seems God always has had to hit me over the head in order to get my attention and then give me a swift kick every so often, to keep me on my toes. But, somehow, it got through this thick skull of mine that I needed to be baptized.

Yes, I had been "dunked" when I joined my first church, but I had not trusted Christ as my personal Savior at that time. Someone described Baptism to me like this: "It is like putting the wedding band on the finger AFTER you are married to show the world that you belong to the person to whom you are married. Baptism is a beautiful picture to show the world that you belong to Christ."

Not long after my baptism, the Lord began to deal with my Mother's heart. One morning as we sat in Church singing "Just as I am," I looked up and saw Mother walk down the aisle and trust Christ as her personal Savior. I was so happy I felt as if my heart would burst. Now, all that remained was Daddy, and my younger brother and sister. I had a new hope and could pray with much more confidence that I had never been able to do in the past.

Within a few years, my father came to trust Christ while away from home on a business trip. Then my sister, Elaine at the age of 9 asked Christ to come into her heart and surrendered her life into full time Christian service.

One by one my entire family were ~~beginning~~ becoming Christians. Now, all that was left was my baby brother. One day, as he was walking in the garden with Daddy, Ralph also trusted Christ, as Daddy told him how Christ had died for him and would take him to heaven one day, if he would only ask Him to. Sometimes, I am so overwhelmed by the Grace and Mercy of the Lord that I can hardly believe it.

As the song says, "God is truly so GOOD!!!"

Now my whole family was saved and on their way to Heaven with me, what more could any person ~~as~~ ask for? Well....I always managed to think of something.

All the rebellion that I had never surrendered to the Lord always kept tripping me up in my walk for Him. I tried to live for Christ and love people the way He said to, but I must admit I was never quite successful. I decided to approach life from the negative angle. I would put on my beautiful Pharisee robe and do nothing. Everything was a sin! I hated everything so much, that pretty soon I even hated ME!

My parents were so patient with me and my many moods. They too, were searching to find God's will for their lives. They would listen to the conflicts that were taking place in my heart and were actually afraid to tell me what to do for fear it might not be the right thing. So I just blindly pushed ahead, not knowing or stopping to think where the road I was taking might lead.

CHAPTER V
LEAVE OF ABSENCE

Revelation 2:4...."Nevertheless I have somewhat against thee, because thou hast left thy first love."

After graduation from High School, I was offered a job with Delchamps, Inc. in the downtown office. At the time I really believed God had opened the door for me –I have since learned that Satan can open doors too! In fact, I often wonder just how big his "Key Chains" must be; especially for "my doors". It was here that I began noticing how much fun lost people had. They didn't have the HOLY SPIRIT to make their hearts feel so guilty and God wouldn't even punish them because they weren't His children. I temporarily forgot about the judgment they would one day face and decided to join them and pass myself off as "one of the group."

It worked so perfectly, no one even suspected I was a "born again Child of the King". Before too very long, I nearly forgot too!!

I started dating guys from the office, in spite of the fact that I was wearing Mel's engagement ring. Finally, one day I knew I couldn't any longer go on playing – "I led two lives". So I made up my mind which way I wanted to go. I didn't ask God which way He wanted me to go. I suppose I was afraid He might not agree with me.

So, I wrote Mel and told him the engagement, marriage, and whole package deal was off. I didn't want to go to school to study to be a missionary. I was having too much "fun," I just wanted to be free.

Little did I realize that a Child of God can only be free when Christ sets him free. (John8:36, "If the Son, therefore shall make you free, you shall be free indeed) I was weaving myself into a web of sin that would hold me tight for many painful years.

Mel rushed home from school and begged me to reconsider, but my mind was make up. I told Mel that I simply did not love him, I believe somehow with my lost love for him, I forfeited my first love – Christ. I can't say I truly understand it even today. I wasn't taking time to weigh my feelings or actions and the last thing I had on my mind was eternal consequences of turning my back on my Savior. But, when I said good-bye to Mel that day, I also took a "Leave of Absence" from the presence of My Lord.

I had been in Church and read my Bible enough to know I couldn't get away with this game I was playing. But, I was determined to give it a jolly good try. Everything was great in the day time, as long as I was at work and around people. It was those nights! Those long, dark, lonely, empty, scary nights.

I couldn't stop the sweet faithful Holy Spirit from speaking to my heart with verses from God's Word like: Hebrews 12:6, "For whom the Lord loveth He chastened." I knew sooner or later I was in for a good old fashioned whipping. So, I gritted my teeth and hoped it would be later, much later.

CHAPTER VI
PRINCE CHARMING

Psalm 6:2, " Have Mercy upon me, O Lord, for I am weak."

He was sitting there in the brightest, red, convertible with the most beautiful eyes I had ever seen. As a child I used to dream of the prince who would someday come and carry me away with him to a beautiful palace, and we would be forever happy and so very, very much in love. He was tall with thick, black hair and long, lovely eyelashes. Now – here he was sitting right across from me at Johnny's Drive Inn Restaurant. The only change in the dream was that the slick, black had turned into a shiny red Chevrolet.

I was 18 years old and certainly not ready to be swept off my feet to never, never land. I had just had a new perm in my hair and my nails freshly polished. The year was 1962 and magic was definitely in the air.

I was having a coke there with two other girls and never dreamed he would come over to our car. But suddenly, there he stood, leaning over to say "Hello" to us and looking right at ME! I was no pick-up, not even for Prince Charming, so we decided to leave. We drove around for a while, but decided to go back to Johnny's – just to see if they had left yet. As fate would have it he was still there with his two friends. We pretended not to see them as we found a new parking place, but over they all came as soon as the car stopped.

I wasn't sure what to do – I'd never talked to a strange boy before without a proper introduction. But my heart was pounding so – I could not help but tell him my name.

Finally, we said we really had to go. It was getting late and we already made plans to go to a midnite movie. I secretly hoped they would follow us and sure enough – they did! The three of us pretended to be annoyed and wouldn't talk to them when suddenly O.J. (Prince Charming) stepped up to the movie window and paid everybody's way in. Confidently, he grabbed my hand leading me to a seat. I was so stunned I couldn't say anything and was actually very impressed and excited. Nothing like this had ever happened to me before. I'll never forget the movie, Elvis Presley in "Blue Hawaii" – just about the most romantic thing in the world. We only made small talk during the movie and it was over too soon for me. Of course, I acted very cool and nonchalant because that was the thing a "lady" did, but inside my heart kept saying, " This can't be real – he is soo handsome!"

When the movie was over we all went out to get in our own cars and he casually said to me, "What's your phone? I'd like to call you sometime when I'm back in town?" Why, he doesn't even live in Mobile! I'll never hear from him again, but anyway here goes, "344-1074 is my number." He didn't even write it down, he just said "O.K." and left. I could hardly wait to get home to tell Mother and Daddy about this dashing young Prince I had met named O.J..I was afraid they would be mad at me for sort of letting him "pick me up". But they seemed to understand, and I guess nothing I did shocked them anymore.

When we got home from Church the next morning, the phone was ringing and it was HIM! He had remembered my number – A MIRACLE!

CHAPTER VII
FLYING HIGH

Obadiah 4 [1:4,] "Though thou exalt thyself, as the eagle, and though thou set they [thy] nest among the starts [stars], thence will I bring thee down, sayeth the Lord."

Our first date was to play putt-putt gold [golf] and I played lousy. I never was very good at any kind of sports, but I was always willing to accept the challenge to try anything at least once. I guess I knew right from the first, that I had never felt about anybody the way I was starting to feel about O.J. There were butterflies in my stomach when he would just smile at me. It was all very much like you read in fairy tales.

As we began sharing our hopes and plans for the future, I found out he was a Cadet in Navy Flight Training at the Air Base in Pensacola, Fla. Flying was the one thing he wanted to do all of his life. I didn't know the difference between a jet and a propeller driven plane, but I pretended that I understood every word he said about airplanes and flying in the Navy. I knew if he did it, it just had to be fascinating. There he told me that he planned a career in the Navy as a carrier pilot and again, not knowing the first thing of what he was talking about, I managed to act as though this was a wonderful choice of careers....
(Naive are the young!)

Soon he was transferred to Meridian, Miss. And I was so afraid this would mean the end of seeing him, but he continued to come back to Mobile on weekends. In fact, he only missed one weekend the entire time he was stationed there. Every Sunday we would go to church and then he would have to go back to the base.

He never said that he would come back the next weekend or ask me if I had another date, but somehow I always knew he would be back. I did resent him taking me so much for granted without even asking me not to date anyone else. So I decided to show him that I was a busy girl and he did need an appointment. I accepted a date with another guy for the following Friday night, hoping all the while I would not have to go. Sure enough, 7:00 sharp the door bell rang, but instead of my date, it was O.J.

I immediately informed him that I had another date and he should have told me that he was coming. In his usual confident style he assured me that it did not matter that I had accepted another date, he was here now, and I would go out with him- AND I DID!

Our relationship was the kind for which every girl dreams. He was my Prince Charming and I was his Cinderella. We had a beautiful story book romance and finally he swooped me away to live in his Palace. We had only been dating for a very few months, when O.J. asked me to marry him and follow him to the ends of the earth as he flew off in his big, beautiful jet.

I believe we saw each other exactly twelve times before he gave me an engagement ring. At long last, I thought I had found the happiness for which I was so desperately searching, until O.J. informed me that he had been transferred to Kingsville, Texas.

Why that was over a thousand miles away and we still had six months before we could be married. Cadets were not allowed to be married until they received their wings because it was a very rigid school and all their attention was needed there. In my usual manner I protested loudly and O.J. came to the rescue with the idea that we get married secretly.

Our parents would know about our marriage, but no one else. It sounded so exciting and adventurous that I could hardly wait. My mother, however, was not so intrigued with the idea. She informed me that I left to go get married, she would flush all my clothes down the toilet, upon which I informed her that I would go naked! I meant to have MY own way as usual- and I did! I Samuel 15:23, "For rebellion is as the sin of witch craft, and stubbornness an iniquity and idolatry…"

It was my first time to fly and my stomach was one big butterfly. I can remember thinking all the way out to Texas- "What in the world am I doing?" I knew at the time that I had stepped out of God's will for my life, but I just tried not to think about that and just to concentrate on my "love" for O.J.

It was almost like being caught up in some fast whirlwind that had taken my breath away. When I landed, O.J. was waiting at the airport to meet me and the look on his face told me that he had just as many doubts as I did. We both had such terrible pride that neither of us would admit how we were feeling. Of course, we could not have a church wedding, because it was to be "secret", so off we went to the Justice of the Peace. It was really awful, nothing a young "Cinderella" dreams of.

The Court House was old and depressing and the Justice of the Peace spoke hurriedly and very curtly. Somehow, I just did not feel married. It was so different from the way I had dreamed and imagined it would be. This was what my rebellion and self will had cost me, and it was only to be the beginning. Numbers 32:23 "...be sure your sin will find you out."

I heard a preacher say one time that he sowed his wild oats and then prayed for a crop failure, but the Bible says, "whatsoever a man sows, that shall he reap" (Gal 6:7). I can tell you of a surety, that is a very, very, true verse.

The apartment that we came home to was a run down, pitiful excuse for a "home." It had three rooms by an old curtain. The bath tub was one of those antiques up on legs. To say that it was less than I had expected is the understatement of the year. The only excitement there was at night when the tarantulas would come out and I would go into cardiac arrest. I used to sit with a fly swatter in one hand and a can of bug spray in the other with my feet up in the chair. We couldn't afford a television or even a telephone, and the only voice I ever heard was O.J.'s. Up until that time, I had thought my Prince Charming's voice had the sound of many beautiful bells, but now my Glamorous Castle had crumbled and I hated the sound, sight, and thought of my castle, Prince Charming, and especially myself. James 4:9, "Be afflicted and mourn, and weep, let your laughter be turned to mourning and your joy to heaviness."

CHAPTER VIII
YOU ONLY GO AROUND ONCE (TWICE)

II Peter 1: 8-9, "For if these things be in you, and abound, they make you that ye shall neither be barren nor unfruitful in the knowledge of our Lord Jesus Christ. But he that lacketh these things is blind and cannot see afar off, and hath forgotten that he was purged from his old sins."

Looking back now, I know that I should have realized that O.J. was not a Christian. He had told me that he was when we first started dating, and I had believed him because I had so desperately wanted to. I truly think he believed that he was saved and on his way to Heaven, because he had been raised in a Christian home and had always been to church. He knew all the right words and could fool the best of them. Again, I don't believe he was trying to fool anybody, he just thought that was all there was to the Christian life.

Actually, I was the one who was not honest with him. I never told him that I believed that God had called me to the Mission Field and that I was not engaged in attempting to justify escape from that calling. I did tell him about Mel and assured him that I no longer loved him. I just could never seem to tell him the rest of the story. In fact, I put this part of my life in the back of my mind and tried to pretend that I was just being emotional and that God had not really ever called me into full time Christian Service.

O.J. received his Navy Wings on December 13, 1962 and we were remarried on that same day. This time it was in the Navy Chapel by the Chaplain and it made me feel good that at least it was a Man of God to whom we said our vows. Of course, neither he, nor anyone else knew it was the "second time around" for us. It had only been three months since our first trip to the Justice of the Peace and I was still having a hard time believing all this was actually happening to me. I have since learned that this "unusual" beginning was to set the pace in our marriage and there would never be anything "ordinary" about our lives together. O.J. used to tease me and say he wondered if he ever divorced me, if he would have to do it twice. I never dreamed just how close we would come to that before it was over.

Our honeymoon was spent at St. Simons Island, Ga., which was to be O.J.'s next duty station. It was a beautiful place and our apartment was in walking distance to the beach. Eugenia Price describes the breathtaking loveliness of the Island in her three books about the places and its people. I was so preoccupied with "myself" and what was happening to "me" that I never saw the beauty of enjoyed our stay there. I was still madly searching for "my happiness", so frantically, that I never stopped to find it.

I was working as a secretary for Sea Pak Corp. and was offered a job modeling my hands for some advertisement that they were doing. I was terribly flattered and O.J. was very proud of me. My boss was very good to me and very understanding when I would come in late, or spend most of the day crying. No one ever knew what was wrong – I suppose they could guess, but I never told a soul that everything was not "peaches and cream" at home.

It was along about this time, however, that O.J. discovered "Happy Hour" at the Officer's Club at the Naval Base and would forget to come home on Friday nights. I suppose this was when the cold realization of what I had done in my rebellion against my parents and the Lord hit me.

I particularly remember our first Christmas together. We went to Charleston, S.C., O.J.'s home for the holidays. This was my first time to see his home that he had grown up in and also my first time to meet his old friends. There was a big Christmas Party and everyone was there. I kept having the feeling of being "smothered to death." Everyone but me was drinking and the party was wild and crazy like nothing I had ever seen.

Finally, I turned to one of the wives and screamed, "I have to get out of here" – AND I DID! I went home and packed, and took my wedding ring off and said, "This is it"!

I guess the one thing that always stopped me from going was the Lord. I knew that marriage was a once in a lifetime bargain and somehow I would have to stick it out – but HOW!?

We had stopped attending church altogether and spent most of our weekends fighting. I don't believe we could be together more than thirty minutes without bouncing each other off the walls! We really had some lou-lou fights.

GINA GREENE

O.J. announced to me as soon as we were married that I was to be his "Slave," at which time I announced to him that I was not a slave and if anything, he would serve me! I was really keen at throwing things; once I threw a high-heeled shoe at him and the heel stuck in the wall!

Then there was the time I ran into the room and threw myself on the bed and broke into heartbroken sobs. O.J. demanded that I unlock the door – I told him to break it down if he wanted in – and he did! What a shock it was to both of us to be standing face to face, finally he just turned and walked away.

We were two, very immature and selfish kids, each determined to have things his/her own way. I should have been trying, I know, to find God's way, but I honestly believe that I had forgotten that Christ had purchased me on Calvary. This was a part of my life that I just shoved aside and tried, and tried, and tried not to think about. Meanwhile, my whole world was crumbling and the happiness that I had always wanted and searched for, was moving further and farther away.

Then one day, O.J. received orders that he was to be transferred to the Naval Air Station at Lemore, California. How exciting! I felt sure that the change of scenery would do us both good. One thing for sure – it couldn't hurt – but it did!

CHAPTER IX
BEAUTY AND THE BEAST

Psalms 73:22, "So foolish was I, and ignorant; I was as a beast before thee."

I've heard it said that California is the land of delight and everything good is there – but I did not find it to be so. My marriage and whole life was going from bad to worse. O.J. began drinking more and more, and I began crying more and more.

Slowly, I began to tell O.J. of the personal relationship I had felt with Christ at one time, but he would only laugh, and say I did not act like a Christian, and he was right – I did not! My handsome Prince had turned into an ugly toad and his lovely Cinderella had turned into a screaming witch!

I began to fear for my life and was actually afraid to go to bed at night without a light on in the room. I knew that the Bible taught that a Child of God would not go unpunished for his sins, and if God saw that he or she would not come back to Him, that it could mean DEATH! I did not want to die, and I really did not want to live either.

All that I could feel was fear and hopelessness. Many nights I felt Satan in my room actually seeking to take my life and I would bargain with God — "Please let me live a little longer. I promise I will come back to you. Oh, please, please let me live."

Someone once told me that a "Navy wife" becomes one of three things – an alcoholic, a hypochondriac, or a nymphomaniac. I truly believe that if a woman doesn't know the Lord, they are correct in this appraisal.

The men are away from home so much – war games, where they are gone for a few weeks and the cruises that take them away for months and months. It is a lonely, lonely life. You grow so far apart and learn to do things your own way so much that it is very hard to adapt when men come home again.

When the men are home, there are cocktail parties and the social necessities that demand your time. I learned to hate the "social functions" and the mere thought of seeing those miserable faces at another party would send me into a fit of depression.

I did everything I could so to rebel against the Navy and the restrictions it posed on my life, but I learned you can't fight the U.S. Government. When they say do it – you do. I pretended to be ill in order to avoid the coffees and luncheons that the wives had.

I resented them for stealing my time and the Navy for stealing my husband. Still, I demanded to have things MY way. I can see now that God was molding and shaping my life and my will. I was a rough diamond that He was polishing, chipping off the rough edges in order to get that bit of sparkle out of it (and it hurt).

I had left home to find my freedom, but what had I found? More bondage! I had even less to say over my life than I did with my parents. God is so faithful in teaching us our lessons. There is no escape from the awesome power of Almighty God. Only in surrender is victory!

I Corinthians 7:22, "For he that is called in the Lord, being a servant, is the Lord's freeman; likewise also that he is called, being free, is Christ's servant."

I can't remember clearly enough now to say exactly when O.J. began to lose his love for me or when my respect for him began to fade, but slowly over the painful years, it happened. There were good times, but mostly there were the bad ones.

Then one exciting day, I learned that I was pregnant. We had been married for three years and wanted a baby very much. Surely this would be the answer for us! A baby would bring us close together and give us a new love for each other!

Everything was wonderful for about three months, then boom! I lost the baby! It was such a shock to us both. Why, why, why, why? O.J. was heartbroken and I was mad at God.

Didn't God know this was the answer for us, at least that was what I thought. I seemed always to know the answer and to have things worked out the way I thought would be best.

Isaiah 55:8-9, "For my thoughts are not your thoughts, neither are your ways my ways, saith the Lord. For as the heavens are higher than the earth, so are my thoughts than your thoughts."

One week after losing the baby, O.J. was sent to Hawaii to prepare to leave for the war in Viet Nam. It was more than I thought I could bear. The one thing I had always feared was my husband going to war. My father fought in World War II and I did not see how in the world I could live ~~thought~~ through the fear that my mother had experienced.

Then there was the horrible guilt of knowing that I had not been the wife I should have been. I had let so many precious, wasted years go by that I could have been loving and caring for him. Now it was too late.

I felt sure that if he was not killed in the war that surely he would find someone else to love and never return to me. Again I could see what my rebellion had cost me. What was I to do? I had nothing to remember O.J. with and nothing for him to return to me for. The baby that I had hoped would bond us together had died and now there was nothing.

Psalms 73:2-3, "But as for me, my feet were almost gone my steps had well nigh slipped."

CHAPTER X
A TIME OF WAR

Ecclesiastes 3:1-3 & 8, "To everything there is a season, and a time to every purpose under the heaven, a time to be born, a time to die; A time to kill, and a time to heal…A time to love, and a time to hate; a time of war, and a time of peace."

"FOR 333 DAYS SHE NEARLY DIED." That was what one of the local newspapers wrote the day O.J. came home from the Viet Nam war. It sounds a bit like a soap opera, but it is in fact the way it happened.

San Francisco has always been one of the most romantic cities in the world to me. Whenever O.J. would have to go out on the ship for war games, I would always follow him and we would spend a few days sightseeing before he left. Some of the few pleasant memories were on such trips to San Francisco. It seemed only fitting that this would be the place from which he would leave to begin his fight for our Nation.

We drove down in our old faithful Olds and stopped as often as possible to cause the time to go slower. The weather was beautiful, as it always is in San Francisco, and the birds were singing. The ocean was bright blue and everything seemed so alive that you could feel the excitement in the air.

Our men were going to protect our American Dream and we were all very proud of them. No one dared utter the words that kept going over and over in our hearts – "How many of these men will return?"

The ship was an aircraft carrier named the "Coral Sea", and it was so big that I couldn't conceive of how it could float. All the sailors wore their white uniforms, and it was truly a breathtaking picture.

The hours flew by and before we knew it they were sounding the bells for the men to come aboard. We had said good-bye many times, but this was very different. How does one go about saying good-bye when it would be for months, and quite possibly forever?

Some of the wives hung onto their husbands' necks, crying and not caring who saw them. I later learned they were the ones who had to part with their husbands before, in order for them to go on these long cruises. There are no words to express the depth of your feelings as you stand there watching that big ship begin to pull out of the harbor.

I watched O.J. as he climbed to the top of the deck and got smaller and smaller in the distance. Quickly, a group of us wives raced over to the Golden Gate Bridge where the ship had to pass under, hoping to get one last glimpse of our men who was on his way to fight for all of the things that men had been fighting for centuries – Freedom, Liberty and our American way of life.

Somehow, all of that seemed unimportant, as I stood there alone on that bridge. All I could think was that once more my happiness had vanished. Would I ever find that pot at the end of the rainbow or was my search to be totally in vain? I did not know what course to take now. I knew that I had married O.J. in rebellion, but I sincerely loved him and believed he loved me. Now he had gone, and I could not be sure if he would ever return. Loneliness, despair, hopelessness and utter confusion were my only feelings. I don't remember how long I stood there that day, but at last the Coral Sea and all the men aboard her were just a speck on the horizon.

Looking for some kind of direction in my life, I decided to go back home to my mother and father and wait for O.J. to return. They were very good to me and really tried to understand what I was going through, but I really don't believe anyone in Alabama could feel the situation like the people who were involved in it.

I took a job to help pass the time, but found myself listening to the radio for any news of the war, so much so, that I could not keep my mind on my work. Every avenue seemed a dead end and I was even more miserable than I had been before.

I tried getting active in church again, but all I could see was that all my old friends had husbands to sit with. I did not fit in with the wives and I certainly did not fit in with the singles. The time dragged by and the days were a week long, until finally it was Christmas.

I had hoped and hoped that O.J. would be able to call me on Christmas Eve, but he did not. Instead I received a crumbled orchid in the mail that I wore on my bathrobe all day because I was too depressed to go out. I could not possibly have known the personal "hell" that caused O.J. not to call me on that day.

I was later to learn that he had gone ashore with several other men from the ship to celebrate the holidays. They began drinking and before long had lost all track of time and reality. Thirty-six hours later, O.J. awoke to discover that he had no idea of where he had been or what he might have done. As he looked into the mirror that evening he saw staring back at him a 24 year old alcoholic! The realization of his appalling predicament led him to a life changing decision. NO MORE ALCOHOL! This was the turning point in O.J.'s life. At the time I did not realize that he was just as miserable as I was and a lot more frightened.

Knowing May 29th was the day that the ship was to return to San Francisco, I kept a calendar and marked the days, not counting the day he would come home or the present date, so as to cut off two days. We wrote every day and one letter stands out in my mind particularly. There was a piece of metal in it about the size of a marble. It was a bullet that had hit O.J.'s plane and sent him into a spin that only the hand of God could have stayed! It was a miracle and O.J. knew it.

I sent him a bible and he started carrying it on his combat missions with him. Slowly he began attending church services aboard the ship and his shipmates began to notice a difference in him. The wives would tell me little stories that their husbands would write home about him.

I could hardly believe my ears, even the tone in his letters began to change. He spoke of God often and really began to depend on Him for a safe return home. I did not know or understand the conflicts or turmoil-taking place in O.J.'s heart, but I was thankful that at long last the cold, self-sufficient personality was learning to depend on someone other than himself.

A few days before the ship was due to arrive, I drove to California to find a house and to prepare for O.J.'s return. It was a long trip from Alabama to California because I only drove during the day. Count, our family dog, was my travelling companion. It was an exciting journey for me, however, as each day brought me closer to our new beginning as husband and wife.

I arrived in ~~Lemoore~~ Lemore, California just in time to get the news that the ship has been delayed and would not return until November 3. That was FIVE months away! Panic and disappointment filled my heart! I had just driven 3,000 miles to meet my husband that I had not seen in six months and now it would be even longer! I did not know which way to turn. My parents wanted me to come back home, but I longed to be surrounded with my own things and with the furniture O.J. and I had shared. It was no fun finding a house and moving in alone, but I knew it was my only alternative.

Most of the other wives lived in the same small community and we had each other with whom to share our loneliness. The war and "our" men fighting it was the only topic of conversation.

One afternoon as we all sat chatting, one of the wives ran home to get her swimsuit. A dip in the pool had seemed a pleasant change of pace for us. She was taking so long, that I decided to check on her. As I stepped into the yard I could see a huge black car parked in her driveway. It was the Navy Chaplain and Commander of the Naval Air Station. They had come to deliver a telegram telling Sue that her husband had been shot down and killed. This was to be only the beginning – day after day we would hear of another friend that had either been killed or captured! "Will O.J. ever come home to me", I wondered? "Will this horrible war ever be over?"

One day the news on the radio said that three A4C Skyhawk jet bombers had been shot down over the South China Sea. Unusually, they listed the names, but today they did not. My pulse raced as I held my breath, knowing it was O.J.! I decided I could not stand wondering any longer so I phoned Ken McAlhany, O.J.'s best friend in Washington, D.C. He was in the Navy there and could find out for me right away. "I can't tell you who it is", he said, "but it's not him"! I had such a feeling of relief that I hung up nearly forgetting to say "thank you".

I knew I had to find something to occupy my mind. I found a little church nearby and began teaching a class of 14 year old girls. It was really a blessing to me and caused me to see that even though I had turned my back on Christ, He is always willing to forgive. I had very little knowledge of the scriptures, but teaching this class was the beginning of my revived search for God's will in my life.

Slowly the long days, weeks and months passed and now it was finally October. The closer O.J.'s homecoming came the more I feared what it would be like. I could barely remember what his eyes were like and how his voice sounded. It had been nearly a whole year since I last saw him! How would he feel about me after all that time? Would we be just two complete strangers? These were frightening thoughts!

Two days before the ship was to pull into harbor, it was announced that the pilots would fly in ahead of the ship. Why, that was tomorrow! Quickly I put all the last minute touches on the house, clean sheets, flowers on the table and a big sign that read "Welcome Home."

I had been sewing on a new wool cranberry suit for weeks and all that remained to be done to it was the final pressing. I shampooed my hair, polished my nails and then went to bed, hoping to be able to sleep. It was impossible! Tomorrow, my husband was coming home!

All of us wives gathered at the hanger early, hoping to be the first one to see or hear the planes as they flew in. The minutes were like hours and it seemed the planes would never appear. Finally, someone saw a tiny speck above the clouds! Soon the sky was filled with big, beautiful, blue jets! It was them! Our men were coming home from the war!

As the planes began to land I tried to find O.J. One by one the men climbed out and the wives ran to meet their husbands. Where was O.J.? There was only one left, was that him? He was so thin and walked bowed like an old man! As he removed his helmet I could see that it was O.J. Would he be able to recognize me? Oh, what agony! After what seemed like an eternity, our eyes met, and yes, yes, YES! All the months of waiting and worrying seemed to vanish in that one moment – there he was – ALIVE!

We were running now! We could not hold each other tight enough. How do you make up for a year in one squeeze? That was what we wanted to do. I don't know how long we stood there just looking at one another, but it was a very long time. There was a band playing and drums beating so loud that we couldn't understand a word that was being said. People were making speeches and trying to scream above all the noise. O.J. rubbed my arms so much that the knap on my jacket rolled up and completely ruined the wool. I didn't notice it that day, but later I cried happily as I saw it.

We talked so much that our jaws ached during the next few days. Even though we had written to each other every day, there was so much that couldn't be said in a letter.

O.J. really believed that since God had answered his prayers and brought him home safely and since he no longer smoked or drank, that he must now be a Christian. He began attending church with me and we were determined to make our marriage a good one. Though we tried desperately we were not successful because "Except the Lord build the house, they labor in vain that build it" (Psalm 127:1)

CHAPTER XI
IT'S A GIRL

Psalm 127:3, "Lo children are an heritage of the Lord: and the fruit of the womb is his reward."

We've got it! This is finally what I always dreamed marriage would be like. We truly love each other and nothing can ever separate us again. We will be like the fairy tale romance says and "live happily ever after."

We began attending church together and it was beautiful. I was teaching 14-year-old girls and O.J. was in the Pastor's class. It was just the way I had planned, until one Sunday morning the rafters came crashing down on my head!

The Preacher called on O.J. to pray in the church service. He nearly passed out on the spot! Afterwards he told the Pastor never to ask him to pray in church again. O.J. did not know what to say and was very embarrassed. But I must admit he wasn't nearly as embarrassed as I was! I had been so proud of his prayer, it seemed perfect to me, but I couldn't bear the thought of that preacher knowing that my husband was not thrilled to lead in prayer or do any other job in the church.

This sort of tarnished my golden dream somewhat, but I was able to pass it off in time and just tell myself that it was merely because

O.J. was such a new Christian. But things of this sort kept coming up all the time. Slowly, we began to drop out of church and keep to ourselves. We didn't enjoy being with the old drinking Navy crowd, but it was a little uncomfortable around the church crowd too.

About this time O.J. made his decision to leave the Navy and apply with the airlines for a job. He began sending resumes to the different companies and they all seemed to be hiring. One of them particularly caught our attention, Delta Air Lines. We heard nothing but good about the company and we especially liked the cities that we would be able to live in if O.J. was employed with them. So, Delta was the one that O.J. chose to pursue.

Even though I believed my prayers had been answered, I knew something was terribly wrong, still I kept telling myself that it was the war and both O.J. and I had a lot of adjusting to do. I had prayed and prayed that he would be hired by Delta Air Lines and we could move somewhere new and start all over again.

The days passed and soon it was weeks and months and still no word. Then someone told O.J. that perhaps he should contact Delta. They said that Delta might like to know that he really wanted to go to work for them and not just any airline that would hire him. He decided that was the best thing to do, so he made the call while I began praying harder than ever. Delta sent him a pass to go to Atlanta for the interview and testing and ten days later a letter came saying he had been hired and to report for classes on June 13, 1966. I was so happy, and I knew God had answered my prayers.

To make things even more exciting, I discovered that I was pregnant again. Nothing would happen to our baby this time. The doctor had said that many young women lose their first babies, now I would have no trouble. Things were beginning to take a turn, and now we would truly have our new life.

O.J. and I were bubbling over with joy. We were like children with a new toy, the prospect of a new job and a new baby made our days full. Then, all this suddenly came to a crashing end as I began to have difficulty with my pregnancy and the doctor ordered me to bed. I still had hope, until one night about 2:00 a.m. I awoke with severe cramps. O.J. rushed me to the hospital and I had to have a D.N.C. I was very depressed, but I managed to say that I had given it to the Lord. I knew the time wasn't right, but would the time EVER be right for us to have a baby?

We left California and moved into an apartment in Jonesboro, GA. It was a small two bedroom, furnished one. I had nothing to do but THINK. I wanted to do something with my life, but did not know what was wrong and how to go about solving the problem.

We lived there three months while O.J. was in school with Delta. There were several other couples living there that were in training with the airlines also. I enjoyed them but O.J. had to study so much that there wasn't much time for social graces, so I just kept to myself again.

The long days and weeks finally came to an end, and it was time to find out the place where we would be sent to live permanently. We just knew it would be Atlanta. We were so sure in fact, that we had begun looking for a house and put a down payment on one. I just knew this was our new beginning. We would have our "Castle" at last.

No sooner had I gotten excited then O.J. came in with the news of our new home, but it was not the one I had in mind. We were to be moved to Dallas, Texas! What in the world was happening to us? Was God trying to punish me? Dallas was SO far away, and I wanted to live in Atlanta so that we could be near our parents. Surely, that wasn't a selfish motive. But, still here it was –Dallas, Texas.

Grudgingly, I packed the few things we had and tried to adjust my thinking to moving so far away. Well, maybe it won't be so bad. Maybe this is the place we will find our ultimate happiness. They say everything is big in Texas; maybe our "joy" will be big too. HA!

We decided to buy a house and not throw any more money away on rent. We really had to pinch our pennies because O.J. had taken a big pay cut when he left the Navy. That was a long way from where we had started at $45.00 per month, but still we had to be very frugal.

We finally found a house that we could move into for nothing down. We were able to buy it VA and got a very good bargain. It was our first real home and I was so excited about making curtains and fixing it up.

Then we learned that once again I was pregnant. This was my third pregnancy. I was afraid to get my hopes up this time, but I could hardly conceal my excitement.

We decided to go to Charleston for a few days to see O.J.'s parents and tell them the good news. What started out to be a delightful trip turned into a fiasco. We both wanted a baby so badly, but we just couldn't seem to get things going for us. We would fight over everything. When we were alone in the car was the worse time. It seemed we couldn't agree on anything. If I said it was hot, O.J. said it was cold.

The main thing we seemed to argue about was the Bible. O.J. would keep calling me "Miss Holy" and asking me questions like where did Adam and Eve's sons get their wives. He could have cared less – it was just something he knew I couldn't answer.

Our visit to Charleston turned out to be more than a few days. Once again I began having trouble with my pregnancy and was ordered to bed. By this time, I believed God was mad at me and punishing me for my rebellion – Psalms 107:11-12, "Because they rebelled against the words of God, and condemned the counsel of the most High; Therefore he brought down their heart with labor; they fell down, and there was none to help."

But, how to get out of this mess was impossible for me to see. I prayed and prayed, but it seemed my prayers never were heard. Then, one morning while O.J. was out shopping for a few groceries I began to hemorrhage. I had never seen so much blood in all my life and I was afraid I would die before I could see O.J. again.

The doctor kept looking for tissue to be sure the baby was dead before he would take me into surgery. I knew the baby could not possibly be alive after all that blood, and I just prayed he would not wait too late. After what seemed hours to me, he told the nurse to take me up to surgery. Still O.J. had not arrived. Everyone was calling him and looking for him, but he could not be located. Later, he told me that he had gone back home with the groceries, not suspecting anything was wrong and walked into the bathroom to find the shock of his life. Blood was everywhere, on the towels, floor and even walls. He rushed to the hospital as quickly as he could, but they had already taken me into surgery.

When I awoke, O.J. was looking down at me and I suppose we were both thinking the same thing. WE WILL NEVER HAVE A BABY! To make matters worse, the doctor came into the room about that time and told us that he had found something wrong in my uterus, and that I must have it corrected with surgery before I could ever hope to have a baby. However, he added unless it was a skilled surgeon it would cause my uterus to tear when it was enlarged in pregnancy.

Now the future looked very dark. I wanted a baby so badly, and I knew O.J. wanted one even more than I did, if that were possible.

I underwent all the tests available to try and discover what was wrong with me. I felt fine and just couldn't understand why I was having all the problems. To my amazement, when the results of the tests came back, they were not able to find one thing wrong! I was normal in every way. I believe this was the first time the hand of God reached down and touched me personally. I knew I had been healed! It was a miracle! Dare I hope that we might be able to have a baby after all? Maybe this was God's way of saying "it's all right now."

Later we discussed this with my doctor and decided to try once again. This time we would have to do things differently. O.J. had to do all the housework for me and that was awful – but we managed. It was so hard to remember to lay around when I felt so good. Then the doctor started me on routine injections of hormones. It was usually around the fourth month that I began having trouble, and as that month approached I became more and more anxious.

In the meantime, we found a wonderful church in Irving, Texas, the little suburb of Dallas where we had bought our home. There were several couples our age with no children there, and we all seemed to have a lot in common. O.J. began trying to be a "good Christian" once more.

He paid his tithe, attended all the services and even witnessed to people. On the outside, there was not a finer Christian man anywhere. But, there was still something that I could not put my finger on. His heart never seemed to change. He begrudged giving his money and seemed to enjoy the fellowships after church more than he did the services themselves.

One day we had a famous evangelist come to the church and everybody was getting their lives right with the Lord. In one of the meetings O.J. went down the aisle and announced that he had been saved in Viet Nam and wanted to be baptized. He gave a brief word of testimony after which I thought my heart would burst! My baby would have the Christian home I had prayed for, for so long. God had truly forgiven me and was once more answering my prayers!

My stomach grew and grew and finally I had to begin wearing maternity clothes. O.J. was so proud and our fighting came to a temporary truce.

The Naval Reserves had always been a "dirty word" in our home, but O.J. was beginning to talk about it more and more. With a new baby, came added expenses and he would make enough in the Reserves to buy the house we both really wanted to bring the baby home to.

I hated the thought of him flying those single engine jets again, but he was so determined to join the Reserves that I had no choice but to give in and tell him to do it if that was what he wanted. He assured me that there was no chance of his getting recalled, because the President had not done that in years. So I accepted his assurances and focused my thoughts on the baby-to-be.

However, this started a new point of contention with us and we began to argue as much as before. There just seemed to be nothing we could agree on once more. I just told myself it would be different when the baby came.

Early one morning I began to have labor pains and it was still two months before the baby was due. It can't be – but it was! O.J. rushed me to the hospital where the doctor was waiting. He assured us that the baby would live if it did come early, but he wanted to avoid that if at all possible. They began giving me hormone injections every time I had a labor pain. After about 18 hours, the contractions stopped and I went home. Now I had to be even more careful than before. Each *hour* our was a day long, each day a week, and each week a month long. We had the nursery decorated in red and white. This baby was to be different and it had to have something different surrounding it – none of that old blue or pink like ordinary babies have.

I promised the Lord if He would let us have a healthy baby that I would give him or her back to Him. I suppose I felt a little like Hannah when she prayed and asked God to give her a child and He gave her Samuel. I Samuel 1:11, "And she vowed a vow and said, O Lord of hosts; if thou wilt indeed look on the affliction of thine handmaid, and remember me, and not forget thine handmaid, but wilt give unto thine handmaid a man child, then I will give him unto the Lord all the days of his life."

But without reason I secretly asked the Lord for a girl. I didn't tell anyone except the Lord, because I knew I would love and be thrilled no matter which the Lord saw fit to give us.

Elaine, my sister was visiting with us that summer and she would bring all the neighborhood young people in to watch the baby move in my stomach. It was such a miracle of life to all of us. On the surface we were happy, gay, and loving. We always managed to wear our masks. Not one person ever guessed the horrible turmoil we were going through. I lived in constant fear that something would be wrong with the baby and I believe O.J. did too. But it was never discussed aloud. We were afraid to admit our thoughts and fears even to ourselves.

One evening as I lay on the sofa I began to have contractions just like the ones I had three months earlier. "THE BABY!! I believe it is time." That was all I could say. O.J. started running around the house getting my suitcase and yelling at the top of his lungs giving everyone orders. "Call the Doctor!" "Get the car!" "Do something!" I'll never forget how excited and upset he was. He didn't even want me to get dressed.

As it turned out we had plenty of time. My labor lasted 12 hours. The baby was big and was turned sideways so I had to push it straight. The doctor let O.J. stay in the labor room with me until the last minute when they wheeled me into the delivery room. I was still awake and SCARED!

After what seemed a very long time the doctor held the baby up for me to see. It was a GIRL! "Is she alright? Does she have all her fingers and toes?" I asked. "Yes," the doctor assured me, "She is perfect." "Oh, the Lord is so good!" That was all I could say and that was enough! I Samuel 1:27-28, "For this child I prayed and the Lord hath given me my petition which I asked of him: Therefore also I have lent him to the Lord; as long as he liveth he shall be lent to the LORD."

When the doctor brought the baby out to O.J. for him to see, he could hardly believe it. I suppose he was the happiest, proudest father in the whole world. He began skipping down the halls of the hospital and singing, "I have a daughter, I have a daughter." Elaine told me later that she was actually embarrassed, but he just could not contain his emotions.

We had agreed on the name Tiffany Koren and decided to call her Tiffany. That means "little jewel" and that was just what she was. I had never seen anything more beautiful and delicate. I wasn't sure how to hold her and it scared me to be alone with her. I was so afraid something would happen and she would be taken from us. After five years of waiting and three painful miscarriages we had our beautiful baby at last! The Lord knew just the right time and just the right place and just the right everything. I knew that I purposed in my heart to be a better Christian for Him.

CHAPTER XII
HERE WE GO AGAIN

Psalm 13:1-2, "How long wilt thou forget me, O LORD? Forever? How long wilt thou hide thy face from me? How long shall I take counsel in my soul, having sorrow in my heart daily? How long shall mine enemy be exalted over me?"

She was the healthy, adorable little girl I had secretly prayed for. Tiffany was really a very good baby. The only problem we both had was my being an over-cautious mother. I wouldn't give her a ~~change~~ *chance* to cry for anything, because I was standing over her just waiting to see if she might possibly need one thing. I couldn't enjoy her like I should have because I worried so much about her. But we had a close relationship even when she was an infant in my arms. Everything was just the way I dreamed it would be until she was three months old.

I was doing my morning exercises in front of the T.V. with Jack Lelane when the phone interrupted me. It was one of the men from the church inquiring as to whether or not I had heard anything about the recall of the Naval Reserves. "No!" I assured him that he must be mistaken. O.J. hadn't called and, of course, he would know if there had been a recall. I was a little shaken, but decided to go on with my routine as usual. Just about the time I had managed to convince myself that everything was all right, the television program was interrupted with a news bulletin.

THE PRESIDENT HAD RECALLED THE ~~NAVEL REERVES~~ NAVAL RESERVES AND O.J.'S SQUADRON WAS ONE OF THOSE HE HAD NAMED TO GO ON ACTIVE DUTY. It can't be! I told myself it was a mistake. There was a terrible battle taking place in my mind when my thoughts were again broken by the ringing of the telephone. This time it was O.J. and he knew nothing of all the chaos taking place across the nation. He was in between flights, just called to say hello, and see how Tiffany and I were doing. I pleaded with him to tell me that there was a terrible mistake, and he was very convincing since he truly believed it was just a rumor. However, while we were still talking another pilot came up to him and broke the news that he was indeed one of the men who had been called onto active duty.

There are no words to describe my feelings at that moment. I felt the Lord had completely abandoned me. Things were just beginning to be right for O.J. and me. We were so happy with the new baby and new house and now the bottom had fallen out again. It seemed every time things began looking up, something came along and knocked my feet right out from under me.

Looking back now, I understand that the Lord could not possibly allow all the things I thought I so desperately wanted. I had never surrendered my stubborn will and all these disappointments were designed to assist me in doing this. But instead of using these opportunities to give God the glory and surrender to Him, I resisted with my whole being and demanded the Lord change things to comply with my wishes. Oh, praise His dear name that He knew best for me and did not give in to my pleadings.

It was several months before the squadron was moved to San Diego, California. We had to sell the TR-4 that O.J. had bought while on cruise in Japan and drove out in a new white station wagon. We had driven the same roads many times during the earlier years of our marriage and it brought back bitter memories. But, this time we had the baby with us and I tried to concentrate on her. It was pretty futile, however. I was filled with hatred for the Navy and even for President Johnson.

How dare they do this to me!, I thought. O.J. had already served his time in Viet Nam and now they were sending him back into war again. There were plenty of young men who had never been the first time. It just wasn't fair- and I told everyone I came in contact with! O.J. really was a bit excited, I believe, to be serving his nation once more, but I made life hell for him. Every time we tried to talk I yelled at the terrible injustice of the government. I know it was a very trying time for O.J. as well as for me.

I demanded that he call my parents and find a house near them that Tiffany and I could buy as soon as he left for Viet Nam. I just knew that he could not possibly live through <u>two</u> wars! So at least <u>that</u> problem would be solved and I would not have to move after hearing the fatal news of O.J.'s death or capture.

I could have been such a witness to the other wives in the squadron and to my new neighbors, but instead I just cried! I wouldn't go to any of the coffees the wives had because they were drowning their grief in Bloody Mary's, and martinis. I couldn't bear their flippant attitudes and I had no idea of how to cope neither with their despair nor with my own.

The men drank more than their wives and I lived in constant fear that O.J. would begin drinking again. The skipper and most of the other pilots would make fun of O.J. for not joining in at "Happy Hour", but by some miracle he never did. I believe that would have been the end of our marriage and quite possibly the end of me if he had. The Lord knows just how much we can take and always stays His hand when we reach that point.

For the first time in my life I asked the doctor for a prescription for tranquilizers. I did not take them often, but sometimes I had to have them just to sleep at night. People had told me that I would love San Diego. It is a tropical environment and stays around 70 degrees year round. I could see nothing pretty about the place. To me it represented heartache and loneliness.

I suppose I cried most of the time, but still I refused to give it to the Lord. I felt in some strange way that He was punishing me for all the years of running from His will for my life, so why should he help me now? Then one morning I could go on no longer. It had been over a year and I had finally come to the end of myself.

As Tiffany and I sat down for lunch, all the hate and fear and despair came crashing in on me and I began to cry and agonize with God in a way I had never done before. I knew that if I continued in this pattern of thinking that I would go insane and quite possibly lose my daughter, one of the few things that really mattered to me. I completely gave up and told the Lord that He would have to do it for me.

I don't have any idea how long I prayed and agonized with the Lord, but while I was still praying the phone rang. I reluctantly walked over to answer it. The voice on the other end was so excited that I could not recognize it at first, "Have you heard? They are going to release the Naval Reserves. We can go Home."

It was one of the other wives. I just couldn't believe it. O.J. was out on the ship now preparing to leave for the long cruise to Viet Nam. Dared I hope that this wasn't just another silly rumor with no truth in it? Then suddenly I remembered my prayer of only a few moments earlier. "Lord it's in Your hands now." What wonderful, loving, capable Hands! Why hadn't I been able to give it to Him fifteen months ago? I don't know if it would have changed anything as far as the length of time we had to wait and all the other horrible nightmares, but one thing I know, it would have given me peace to endure it.

Someone once said ,"Without the rain, there would be no rainbows." How very, very true that is. I thought for sure my heart would burst before O.J. could get home.

When O.J. walked in the door, I don't know what he thought he would find, but what awaited him was a very happy and grateful wife. O.J. was not the only one who had been "released" that day!

Psalm 107:13-14, "Then they cried unto the LORD in their trouble and he saved them out of their distress. He brought them out of darkness and the shadow of earth, and brake their bands in sunder."

CHAPTER XIII
HE TOUCHED ME

Psalm 28:7, "The LORD is my strength and my shield; my heart trusted in him, and I am helped; therefore my heart greatly rejoiceth; and with my song will I praise Him."

I know now that this was the turning point in our lives. As much as I hated the Navy and all the things that it represented to me, the threats I felt it imposed on my life, this recall was the thing the Lord used to get us back to the place He wanted us.

Delta said that O.J. could move back to Atlanta if he so chose and the Navy paid all of our expenses to move us there. We could never have afforded to make such a big move otherwise. We discussed it and decided that we would to Atlanta and live in an apartment until we could find our dream house and buy it.

We drove back to Georgia singing and laughing as only people who have been under great oppression and duress can after they have been released. Even Tiffany sensed our joy and joined in the gaiety. It was a wonderful trip and I saw so many beautiful sights I had missed seeing before. It's rather funny how our attitudes affect our eyesight.

We spent every afternoon on the road looking for a house and all the rest of the time I spent calling on the phone and looking in the paper for one. We didn't get to know anyone in the apartment complex with us because we were away so much.

When I discovered that I was pregnant, I assumed that I would have no trouble since I had carried one baby to full term. However, that proved to be a mistake. I don't know if it was because I did not take care of myself the way I should with so much riding or if the Lord just knew the time was not right. Anyway, as usual I noticed some spotting in my third month. I had no neighbors I could call on, so we just had to wait for O.J.'s parents to come to help with Tiffany. Finally, one night it became clear that it was no use prolonging it. We called the doctor and asked him to meet us at the hospital.

Once again I had to fight the old depression that came after each miscarriage. It was some better this time because at least I did have one child, but O.J. and I both had wanted a large family with about 5 or 6 children. My body had to become accustomed to living without the large doses of hormones that I was required to take during each pregnancy. It was always a very lonely and empty time for me.

Then one afternoon the real estate agent who had been showing us houses told us about one that would be coming available in a few days. As soon as we drove by, we knew this was the one! We could hardly wait to see the inside.

We still had a house to sell in Dallas and a lot on Lake Spivey that we would have to sell to raise the money required to buy this one in Stone Mountain.

O.J. made a call to an old friend in Irving and she said she believed she knew someone who was interested in buying our house right now. Sure enough the next day she called back and said they were willing to pay our asking price. Praise the Lord! Then we placed an ad in the paper to see the lot and people began calling and actually making bids to buy it. I knew the Lord's hand had to be in it. Things like this don't just accidentally happen.

As soon as we walked through the new house we knew it was the one! We started proceedings immediately and were able to move in right away. The house was beautiful and had so much room! The neighbors came over the very first day and offered to help with Tiffany and in any other way they could. It wasn't long before I learned that most of them were Christians. I couldn't believe it! The Lord had placed us exactly where He wanted us.

As much as I loved my new home and neighbors there was something missing. Again, I found myself unable to find the solution to our problem. I began to think possibly we had made a mistake in moving back to Atlanta and that we should go back to Dallas to our old friends and church. We felt lost in this large city and the people were not as friendly as they were in Dallas. We visited church after church looking for something. I say something because I really don't know what it was we were looking for.

Meanwhile, our little angel daughter was getting to be more than a handful. She was so active; I had to put everything away to keep it from getting broken. I remember particularly her second Christmas. I struggled with myself about whether or not to put up a Christmas tree, knowing it would be turned over and all the ornaments broken. Finally, I decided on a small table size that would not be so tempting. I believe it lasted one hour. I had only two table lamps and she managed to overturn one of them and shatter it. I was so exhausted from chasing Tiffany all day that before dinner time I had to lie down.

It was impossible for O.J. to understand. I had always prided myself on my housekeeping and now I could not have been more disorganized. I just opened the cabinets and threw the canned groceries in, and I kept all the extra cereal in the dishwasher. The house was in constant disorder. I just could not get on top of it. I hated the mess, but I was so tired all the time that I figured that keeping Tiffany from killing herself or ME was first on my list of musts.

My Mother told me that I should spank Tiffany and get some discipline in her life, which I realized was true. But, every time I spanked her I felt guilty. O.J. was as baffled with the situation as I was. We both loved our daughter so much that we believed that we "just couldn't possibly" BEAT her.

Then a miracle happened! My old prayer partner, Edna Hogue from Irving, Texas came to visit us and saw the dilemma we were in. She recommended some good books by Christian doctors on discipline for us to read. That was the turning point in Tiffany's life. I learned that we had to spank her if we did love her. Proverbs 13:24, "He that spareth his rod hateth his son; but he that loveth him chasteneth him betimes."

We would spank her and she would cry and cry, but we were determined to try and raise her the way God planned. We both wanted the happiness and blessings for Tiffany that so far we had failed to find for ourselves. Proverbs 23:13-14, "Withhold not correction from the child, for if thou beatest him for the rod, he shall not die. Thou shalt beat him with the rod, and shalt deliver his soul from hell."

We finally found a church that we felt led to join. It was a young neighborhood church and all the people were friendly. But after a few months we began to realize that there was still something missing, we just knew it was! I believe there is a hunger in everyone's soul until he finds God's perfect will for his life. I don't believe there is anything that can fill that longing except stepping into the exact place God has planned for you.

We began to visit other churches looking for that SOMETHING. One Sunday we joined another bigger church. We thought here we would fit in and end our search for joy, happiness, peace or whatever one calls that yearning that pulls you on. We attended that church for about one year and never felt whatever it was we wanted to feel. We just didn't seem to belong anywhere. Moving back to Dallas seemed to be the best thing to do. So we planned a trip back to see some of our old friends and to see if that felt right. One thing we found out right away, YOU CAN NOT GO BACK!

Everything had changed so much and there were so many new faces, it just wasn't the same. That burst our bubble of moving back. Where did we go from here?

Then one day I realized in all this confusion I had skipped a couple of my menstrual periods and that I must be pregnant again. It seemed I was either always pregnant or just getting over a miscarriage. But this time things were pretty easy for me and I had passed the four month mark before I knew it.

One day when I went in to see the doctor for my check-up, he discovered a fibroid tumor growing in my uterus. "What else can happen?" I asked myself.

I had such a fear of cancer that I knew I could not cope with the thought of living with that thing growing inside of me for months. Dr. Fuerst said that he could do nothing until the baby came, and that he hoped it would not grow to such size as to make me loose the baby.

He added that usually these types of tumors were not malignant. WOW! For me that was overwhelming! Then as usual he told me not to worry, not to get upset, that the important thing was carrying a baby to full term. What an impossible request!

I knew this one was too much for me. So, I decided to do things differently this time- I prayed and gave this problem to the Lord from the first day. I asked Him if He would not heal the tumor to please remove it from my mind so that I would have a chance to carry the baby. I tell you when the Lord does something, He does it just right. I felt the hand of the Lord so real to me. It was as if He touched my heart and said "I am in control. There is nothing to fear." For the very first time in my life, I really believed that.

Psalm 23:4, "Yea, though I walk through the valley of the shadow of death, I will fear no evil: for thou are with me, thy rod and thy staff they comfort me."

CHAPTER XIV
A SON AND A SEARCH

Psalm 43:5, "Why are thou cast down, O my soul? And why art thou disquieted within me? Hope in God for I shall yet praise him, who is the health of my countenance and my God."

"When is O.J. going to be in town for a few days?" Dr. Fuerst asked me. "I am going to induce your labor so that he can be with you when the baby is born." That was one of the things I had prayed for the entire time I was pregnant. Again I could see the Lord guiding my life and coming through for me when I really needed Him.

"Wake up, Mrs. Greene, you have a son." The nurse stood smiling down at me in her crisp white uniform, but I had a hard time focusing me eyes. "A boy!" That was exactly what I had wanted and asked the Lord for! How could He be so good to me? "Is he alright?" "Yes, perfect in every way." "Oh, blessings of blessings. Let me see him." "Oh, I'm afraid you can't see him until morning, the nursery is closed for tonight." Then I knew something terrible was wrong with my baby. They just wouldn't tell me. They were waiting for the doctor to tell me. That was the longest night of my life. When the morning light began to peek over the window sill, I was still praying. Then suddenly I heard the cry of a baby that I KNEW was mine!

A nurse appeared in the doorway, holding a little bundle in her arms and there he was! Otis Jarield Greene, III. Now we had a beautiful daughter and a precious son! I knew that our lives would be perfect and wonderful and all the good things I had always wanted them to be.

I was so excited with the baby that I forgot all about the tumor that had been growing in my uterus. As the doctor explained to me that he was amazed to find NO TUMOR when he delivered the baby, I couldn't keep from smiling. Once more the hand of God touched my body and healed it!

Psalm 40:5, "Many, O LORD, My god are they wonderful works which thou hast done, and they thoughts which are to us-ward; they cannot be reckoned up in order unto thee; if I would declare and speak of them they are more than can be numbered."

Tiffany seemed to adjust to her new brother very nicely. We had all the odds going in our favor. The perfect picture of a happy American family. Mr. and Mrs. Prince Charming and their two darling charmings.

Trey was a typical little boy. He was a happy child; even wet pants didn't seem to bother him. For the most part, Tiffany remained my number one project. She still demanded so much of my attention. Trey seemed to be slower in everything he did than his sister and I counted this as a blessing. It always seemed most important that Tiffany do everything ahead of the books, but with Trey, I had learned to enjoy each new phase and not rush him.

O.J. decided that what we needed to complete our family was a farm, so off we went to search for this perfect Utopia. We convinced some friends that this is what they needed too, so we had someone help us in our searching. I can't tell you how many back roads and mud alleys we rode over during the next few months. I saw more shacks, cows and goats than I ever knew existed in the world. I learned that Georgia was really a farm state and there was more land and creeks and lakes and trees than my mind had ever imagined.

We did have some fun times going over the bumpy roads in our old faithful station wagon. All the adults were in the front and back seats and the kids in the rear. The kids would squeal with delight each time we passed a horse and I just held my breath and hoped we wouldn't find anything too far away from civilization.

I suppose by this time we should have realized that nothing material was going to bring contentment, but we still kept hoping and looking. We knew that even though on the surface we were the ideal family, there was a very big void in all of our lives.

O.J. was flying co-pilot now and his salary had increased enough that we were able to buy most of the things that we had always dreamed of owning. We had a lovely two story home, two new cars and acreage. There was a time in my life I thought, if only we could own our own home I know I would be happy. After the home, I thought if I just had my own car, O.J. is away so much and I might need to go to the doctor or who knows where- now if I just could get that car, I know I would be satisfied. But all those things seemed to fade into non-existence each time we would have one of our three ring fights.

Then, I told myself if the Lord would just give us children, then that was all we needed to complete our lives. Even two perfectly healthy, adorable children were not the answer to the emptiness in our lives.

Nothing that we bought or found or possessed brought happiness! Instead, we began drifting farther and farther apart. I almost began to feel sorry that we had given birth to these beautiful children, because I saw the pain we were inflicting on them. Oh, we never fought openly where the kids could see, but they knew something was wrong. Children sense things when they are not right.

Desperately we tried to find answers. We became very active in our church. I began teaching 14 year old girls and really enjoyed that. Some of the girls became Christians as a result of that ministry. I truly loved them and I believed they loved me. I knew the Bible from front to back and it was always easy for me to tell someone else how to live for Christ. It was applying those teachings to my own life that I found difficult.

Finally I decided to busy myself in my children's lives. I just wouldn't worry about my relationship with O.J. It seemed I had made a mistake in marrying a man who was not a Christian, and even though he professed to be one now, God was just not to bless us and ever allow us to be truly happy. I began to think that I had missed God's will for my life when I did not go to the mission field and now I could not possibly ever find complete peace and joy.

I suppose I decided to settle for "second-best." What a miserable existence. Yes, I knew all the verses that say John 10-10, "I am come, that you might have life and have it more abundantly", but I believed that was only for people who accept God's "first choice" for their lives and respond to His call.

Still I found little satisfaction in just living for the kids. My soul cried for more and more. I began to pray and agonize with the Lord to tell me what was wrong in our lives.

Psalm 14:2, "I cried unto the LORD with my voice; with my voice unto the LORD did I make my supplication. I poured out my complaint before him; I shewed before him my trouble. When my spirit was over-whelmed within me, then thou knewest my part. In the way wherein I walked have previly laid a snare for me.

I looked on my right hand, and beheld, but there was no man that would know me; refuge failed me; no man cared for my soul. I cried unto thee, O LORD; I said, thou are my refuge and my portion in the land of the living. Attend unto my cry; for I am brought very low; deliver me from my persecutors; for they are stronger than I. Bring my soul out of prison that I may praise thy name; the righteous shall compass me about, for thou shalt deal bountifully with me."

CHAPTER XV
WONDERFUL DISCOVERY

Galatians 2:20, "I am crucified with Christ; nevertheless I live; yet not I, but Christ liveth in me; and the life which I now life in the flesh I live by the faith of the Son of God, who loved me and gave himself for me."

"A new hair-do is what I need! I just stay home all the time and change diapers and cook and wash clothes and mop floors and look ugly. I'm either pregnant or just getting or having a baby or miscarriage. I'm not a person any more. Who am I? I'm a maid and a bottle washer! Somehow over the years I've forgotten who I am, or maybe I never knew. I know one thing- I hate my life the way it is!"

"I love my husband, or at least I think I do, but he really is a stranger to me. Come to think of it, I can't remember the last time we had a real conversation." Everything is so surface, "How was your day?" "Fine, and how was your day?" "Fine." Then we both lapsed into periods of screaming at the kids and each other or else we drifted into periods of complete silence. "Even the characters on soap operas have more real existence than I do." I thought.

These were my scrambled thoughts mixed with daydreams and hopes of escape even if escape meant suicide. Everything I had worked for and planned for had failed to give me the happiness I had searched for all of my life. The Lord blessed me more than I dared to ~~imaging~~ *imagine* and yet even the Lord's blessings seemed to lack the power to keep me from the constant depression that tortured my mind. Secretly, I wanted to walk out the door and never look back.

Since I could think of nothing more drastic to do, I settled for a haircut and a new permanent. As I was walking out the door my eye caught a glimpse of a book lying on the shelf that I had never read. "Think I'll take this with me and read it while I'm under the dryer."

After saying the usual nice things to the hairdresser and getting my hair in curlers, I opened the book and began to read. THE TASTE OF NEW WINE by Keith Miller fascinated me as I read that he too had struggled all his life to find "that thing" which would bring him contentment. He said he had given his home and his wife to God and had even surrendered his life to preach. Still he was miserable-something was missing.

Oh, how ~~could I~~ *I could* identify with Mr. Miller! I had done everything I knew to do, said everything I knew to say and prayed every prayer I knew to pray. Mr. Miller went on to say that he finally came to the end of his rope and was ready to give up. One day he was in such a state of mind that he stopped his car along the highway where he was driving and fell on the ground begging God to tell him what the problem was. As I read on my heart was beating so hard and so fast that I knew that everyone in the beauty shop must be looking at me. God seemed to say to him, that He did not want his house, his wife, his money, or even his preaching. All I want from you is YOUR WILL.

"MY WILL"! It took me a little while to absorb the impact of what I had read. My will was the one thing that I had kept locked tightest in the closet of my heart. I planned my life and all the things I wanted to achieve and possess. It had never occurred to me that God must be in complete control in order for all the pieces of my life's puzzle to fit together. MY WILL!!

I must have set there for a long time trying to understand all that I was reading. I knew this was the key! This was what had been missing in my life, the surrendering of my will. Was that why my life seemed to be so up and down? No sooner did I begin to think that things were going pretty good for me than something would come along and push me down into deep despair.

Was it possible to really do the thing that this book kept talking about? I realized now that I must have a very strong will and it would not be easy to crucify it. Still I knew somehow that this was the beginning of something that I had sought all my life. I wasn't sure just how to go about this act of giving my will to the Lord, but I asked Him to help me to learn more about this new life that Keith Miller spoke of. Surely there must be more books written about this or someone could tell me about it.

One Sunday night in Training Union they announced that a young man from Campus Crusade International would be our guest speaker. I sat there expecting it to be boring because he looked so young, but as he began talking I was amazed at what he was saying. He was speaking about this "abundant life" that I had read about only two weeks earlier. His face seemed to glow and it was obvious that he had experienced a new type of life in Christ. He was saying that anyone could possess this joy and peace and it involved one's will.

There was that word again. He held up a little pamphlet with the words "Have you made the wonderful discovery of the spirit-filled life?" written on the front. "No, but I sure want to"! I told myself under my breath. "I am so tired of just living to die, please tell me how to obtain this new life," I almost screamed it out loud!

The young man explained that surrendering one's will was as easy as A B C.

A. Sincere desire to be controlled and empowered by the Holy Spirit, Matthew 5:6 Blessed are they which do hunger and thirst after righteousness: for they shall be filled.

B. Confess your sins. I John 1:9 If we confess our sins, he is faithful and just to forgive us our sins and to cleanse us from all unrighteousness.

C. By faith claim the fullness of the Holy Spirit. Ephesians 5:18 And be not drunk with wine, wherein is excess; but be filled with the Spirit.

So that was IT! It seemed almost too easy. Perhaps I had better think about this a little longer, I thought. Nothing can be that easy.

Next morning I had to be up early to drive the children to kindergarten. I routinely cooked breakfast and dressed to leave. Somehow, I couldn't forget what I had heard the night before. I could still see the young man's smiling face as I dropped Tiffany off at school.

On the way home, I thought to myself, "I can't go through another day like the days I have been going through. I'm ready to try anything." I began to cry for the first time in a very long time and I prayed for the Lord to take my own will and replace it with His. I guess the people riding down the road beside me must have thought I was insane, but I didn't care at that moment. The more I prayed the more excited I became. "Oh, Lord, thank you for letting me in on this mystery! I have longed and ached to know what was wrong with my life! I was beginning to think there was no hope. I give up! You are in control now."

It was like a miracle. I can't explain it; how does one explain a miracle? But something wonderful happened to me in that car that morning. As I opened my eyes it was as if I was opening them for the first time. It was as if I had been in a very dark tunnel with no light at the end and suddenly someone opened a door and beautiful rays of sun came bursting through. I could see things I had never seen before. Dogs and children were running down the sidewalks and planes were flying overhead; all the beautiful sights that make up a beautiful day. The flowers were blooming and the grass was green and the warm rays of the sun made me feel like I could explode with joy!

Suddenly a pain gripped my heart, O.J. How in the world was I ever going to explain this miracle to him? He would never understand it in a million years! He was already beginning to doubt my rationality and this would be the clincher. He would think that this was just another scheme to get his attention. "Oh, Lord, please help me with my husband. I want a Christian home so much and I have failed miserably. Lord, I know I can never be the wife that I ought to be unless you do it for me."

Always before I had prayed for the Lord to save my husband and then we both would serve Him. Now I prayed for the Lord to show ME how to serve Him. I realized that whether my husband was saved or not had nothing to do with my relationship with Christ. I promised the Lord that I was going to live for Him regardless of what O.J. did.

I knew that keeping my mouth shut to O.J. was going to be the hardest part of my new commitment. I loved to preach to him and he hated to see me coming with my Bible in hand. He knew that it usually meant a sermon was coming. But if I couldn't preach to him or even tell about what had happened to me this morning, how was he ever going to know? Then the Lord brought to my mind a verse that says that husbands shall be won by their wive's godly lives.

As I pulled the car into the garage, I could see a neighbor cutting the grass and I yelled to her. "Did you ever see a more beautiful day?"

Psalm 107:2-7, " Let the redeemed of the Lord say so, whom He hath redeemed from the hand of the enemy:…They wandered in the wilderness in a solitary way; they found no city to dwell in. Hungry and thirsty, their souls fainted in them. Then they cried unto the Lord in their trouble, and he delivered them out of their distresses. And He led them forth by the right way, that they might go to a city of habitation."

Malachi:3:7 "Return Unto Me and I will return unto you saith the Lord of Hosts."

CHAPTER XVI
NO MORE SOAP

Hebrews 10:36 "For ye have need of patience, that after you have done the will of God, ye might receive the promise."

"If it weren't for the children, we would get a divorce", O.J. was telling Lee Baugh, our dear friend. I hadn't meant to eavesdrop on their conversation, but I just happened to be walking past the door as they were talking and couldn't help overhearing. Actually, I was beginning to feel the same way. Maybe a divorce would be best after all. We had tried everything in the books and ended up with a big fat nothing.

I could not understand what was happening. I had thought that once I truly gave my will to the Lord that things would be fine, but instead the bottom had fallen out!

Everything had been wonderful for almost two days after my experience with the Lord in the car that day. Then suddenly things seemed to get worse between O.J. and me. What in the world was going on? "I just can't win!" I thought to myself.

Lee and Barbara Baugh had been part of our old crowd in Dallas at our church there. We had taken a few days off to visit them before they left for the mission field. Now here we were spending those last precious moments crying on their shoulders. They were the only two people in the world that had any idea that anything was wrong in our picture-book marriage. Even they were shocked when we shared with them that we did not know which way to turn…It was worse than I had ever imagined it could be.

"Divorce" had always been a horrible word to both O.J. and myself. No one on either side of our family had ever been divorced. Now, here we were on the very brink of having that happen to us!

"I know I must be dreaming, I'll wake up soon and this will all be over." I just could not bear the thought of losing my prince, (O.J.) and yet I knew that we could not continue the way were going. It was tearing us both apart. We both loved the children so much and wanted the right kind of home for them to grow up in, but how to accomplish that was what we could not figure out.

Why was God doing this to me when I had finally surrendered to Him after all those years of running? Was he just being cruel? I prayed and begged Him to patch things up in our marriage and make us love each once more. But, there was no let up.

Since the trip to see Lee and Barb had been such a disaster, we decided to go somewhere alone and try to get reacquainted. Mother volunteered to keep the children so we began making plans to go to Jamaica. It was to be our second honeymoon and a new start.

That was the worst mistake ever! How do two people get to know each other if they can't find anything to talk about. We had become complete strangers, or maybe we were always strangers. At any rate, the colorful island looked drab when my heart was breaking.

We did some shopping in town and looked for things to divert our thoughts, but it proved useless. The beach was alive with shells and tiny creatures that seemed to almost sneer at us as we would walk past, trying to find some type of common interest once more. Everything was futile and we both were more convinced than ever that there was no hope for our marriage.

I did not see how I could go home and tell my family that we were getting a divorce. Then there were the children! "Oh, my God, my God, how can I tell the children!?! Please help me! I know it's not your will for a home to break up, but rather for them to be one in You. Please give us that Christian home! Show me what I can do to help this happen."

Suddenly I thought back to something I had read in Keith Miller's book., "A Taste of New Wine". He had said that he so desperately wanted his wife to feel the way he did and the lord showed him that he must do something that he had refused to do the entire time they had been married. Take out the kitchen garbage! It was a little thing, but it showed his wife that he really was a new person. Was there something that I could do to show O.J. that there really had been a change in my life? I had tried to tell him many times, but he just thought that I was preaching again, so I had stopped trying.

Now I was ready to do anything I could in order to save my marriage. I was finally in the place God had wanted me to be for a very long time. One by one I began giving to the Lord anything that I thought might possibly stand in the way of my relationship with O.J.

I had never been a very submissive wife, in fact I thought that marriage was a 50-50 deal. But I had given those old sins to Christ when I surrendered my will. It was not easy, but I was truly trying to be silent and not preach, what could it be? Then all at once I knew! Of course, it was the "soap operas"! Without realizing it, I had become addicted to them. O.J. hated "As the World Turns", but I always passed it off as his being silly.

"They talk about God", I would justify myself to him. "They are garbage! How can you call yourself a Christian and sit there and watch that trash," O.J. would demand.

Now I suppose it might sound silly to most people but that was a very hard decision for me. My own life had become so rotten that I would look forward to escaping reality for a few hours every afternoon by watching that "garbage."

Right then and there I purposed in my heart that this was the end of the soap operas for me. Instead I would use this time for the Bible Study and prayer that I always found difficult to fit into my busy schedule. I didn't tell O.J. about my decision and I didn't make a big deal about studying my Bible. But when I would put the baby down for a nap I would slip upstairs and have my quiet time with the Lord!

It had been three months since my commitment to the Lord of my will and I could feel His hand on my life in a new way. One morning as O.J. was walking out the door to leave on a trip he yelled back at me,

"Why don't you go to Forrest Hills Baptist Church Sunday morning? You like that sort of church and maybe you will find something there that you need." That was a very strange suggestion coming from O.J., but I knew he was right. That church had always had an appeal to me and I did want to go. "Why don't you go with me?" I asked. "OK...I will sometime." That was all he said, but it gave me hope, the first hope in a long, long time.

Luke 1:37, "For with God nothing shall be impossible."

CHAPTER XVII
A NEW HONEY

II Corinthians 5:17, "There if any man be in Christ, he is a new creature: old things are passed away; behold, all things are become new."

Fall was in the air and I had worked in the yard all day setting out bulbs that would bloom next spring. "Will we still be living together in this house next spring?" I wondered. I was completely exhausted from the yard work and chasing our two very active children all day, but my eyes would not close in sleep. At 11:00 pm I decided to get on my knees and pray for a while to see if that would help bring peace to my restless mind. I still had no idea of what the problem was with my marriage. I wasn't even sure if O.J. was saved or not, but one thing I knew – God knew. All the answers were in His word and if we were ever going to begin putting the pieces back together that was where we had to begin. I prayed and asked the Lord to give O.J. a desire to read His Word and to save him if he was not already a Christian. I had never prayed exactly as I did that night. It was the prayer of a person who knew that she had reached the end of all her dreams.

As the sun began peeping over the tree tops I was still on my knees. Why, I had prayed all night long! How in the world would I ever make it through the day with two small children and all I had to do?

I was sure I would collapse about half-way through. But as the light grew brighter I knew there were two hungry mouths in the next room waiting for me to cook breakfast. I pulled my robe on and slowly made my way down the stairs. Everything looked just the same as it had the night before. Somehow I had expected a difference, but there were the same dirty dishes and wrinkled shirts I had put off doing the night before.

After breakfast and getting the children dressed, I decided to go back out in the yard and work a little while. The time seemed to pass very quickly and before I knew it, O.J.'s car was driving up the driveway.

I actually dreaded to see him come home. What would he have to say to me this morning? And better yet, what would I have to say to him? Surely, I could think of something pleasant that wouldn't cause a fight if I were careful. I was so engrossed with my thoughts that I scarcely noticed him walking toward me.

"Before you say anything I just want to tell you – you have a new Honey." I wasn't sure I had heard him correctly. "I said, that you have a NEW HONEY! Let's go inside so that we can talk." I couldn't believe my ears, O.J. actually wanted to TALK to me? That was a new one! I put down my spade and looked up into his eyes. He was smiling and the lines had disappeared from around his mouth. He had a different expression on his face than I had ever seen before. I knew that something very unusual had happened and I was holding my breath to hear what it was.

I fixed us both a cup of coffee and we sat down at the kitchen table. As O.J. began pouring out his heart to me I saw and heard a person I had never known before – there was, my handsome Prince Charming, My Ugly Toad, my husband of ten years, and a total stranger all at once.

This is O.J.'s story. I asked him to write this chapter because he can tell it so much better than I.

I reported for my flight as usual, but the regular captain was sick and had been replaced with Joe Ivy. I had never flown with him before. The flight was routine from Atlanta to West Palm Beach where we had dinner before going on to Atlanta, Dayton and finally Columbus, Ohio, where we were to layover. We departed West Palm Beach about 10:30 PM…As we flew over Cape Canaveral I asked Joe if I should point out the launch sites. He looked at his watch. "It's only 11:00PM and we just took off, so most of the passengers are awake. Go ahead and tell them."

After making the announcement we engaged in small talk and the subject was generally about the condition of our country. At the time I didn't know why I said it, but I commented that what this country needs to do is get back to good old Bible teaching principles. Joe's comment nearly floored me and I wasn't to know until the next night why he said it. "Amen, brother, how long have you been saved? Tell me all about it?" What in the world did that have to do with the condition of the country? Oh well, he asked, so I'll tell him.

I had told dozens of people about being saved while I was in Viet Nam, I had prayed and asked the Lord to bring me home safely. I had been reading my Bible that Gina had sent me for Christmas. I had come home safely and begun attending church regularly. Tithing became a habit, working with young boys at church, attendance at every service, even being baptized at age 26, I had all the right words to say, but for the first time they didn't make sense.

At this point I need to back up a couple of weeks in time.

Gina has mentioned our church hopping since moving to Atlanta. We had just joined Forrest Hills Baptist Church as a result of our four year old child attending what they called neighborhood Bible Time. It was a summer Vacation Bible School with all the emphasis on Bible verses and songs. Tiffany had been invited to ride on the bus with our friends across the street, George and Mary Wright, and since we knew them well, we let her go.

One afternoon she came home and said, "Daddy, do you know what I learned today?" Tell me what you learned today, Tiffany. She responded with Colossians 3:20 "Children, obey your parents in all things." "Did you hear that Gina? Maybe we should try that church out?" We went to Bible Time closing services that Friday Night, went back on Sunday and then Wednesday and joined the next Sunday.

Several people from the church had been to visit us before we joined and when we went down the aisle we were asked again, "If you died tonight do you know if you would go to heaven?" "Of course," I always answered. I had a great testimony to give which brings me back to where I left off.

We finally made it to Columbus, Ohio and went downtown to the hotel. All the time I couldn't get the fact out of my mind that my story didn't sound right for a change. We had heard this pastor at Forrest Hills, Curtis Hutson, preach four times and he kept talking about the plan of salvation; the Roman Road, death, burial and resurrection; asking Christ into your life, a personal experience. I had heard hundreds of sermons, but none that made it so clear and told how easy it was to be born again.

I wasn't sleepy so I looked for a magazine to read. There wasn't anything in the room to read but a Gideon Bible. I scanned the list of suggested readings in the front and my eye caught the conversion of Saul in the book of Acts. I read that chapter about his trip on the road to Damascus several times trying to digest what it was about. But they kept calling him Paul instead of Saul. I really believed I had found a mistake in the Bible, one for which I had looked many years.

It was past 4:00AM before I went to sleep. I got up about noon and went out to lunch. When I got back to the room I turned on the television but could not get interested in anything. My mind wandered back to the Bible. I picked it up and told myself that all books begin on page one, so I started on page one and read for a while. I couldn't put it down.

All those Sunday School lessons and sermons, and I never realized the ark floated for about a year before the water went down. Everyone knows there were two of every kind of animal in the ark. No one ever told me there were seven of each kind of the clean animals. I didn't know that God told the people in Leviticus that pork was not good to eat or that scavenger animals were not fit to eat.

All these and many, many more were discovered and I was fascinated at the wealth of information I was reading. I had argued with Gina over the least little thing in the Bible and I had never bothered to read it for myself so I could talk intelligently about it. Many of us fall into that category I'm afraid.

We were to meet in the lobby about 5:00pm for the cab ride to the airport for the second day of our flight. At 4:30PM I was still reading. When I realized how late it was I hurriedly shaved and put on my uniform..I picked up my suitcase and headed for the door. It was as if God reached out and grabbed me by the collar and stopped me in my tracks. I felt as if I could hear Him saying to me, "What have I got to do to get you to come to me?"

I put my suitcase down, took off my hat and there in that motel room, all by myself I asked Christ to come into my life as my personal Savior. I told the Lord that I believed that He was virgin born, that he was crucified as my sacrifice for sin, that he arose and that He was coming again, and that I was trusting Him and nothing else to get me to Heaven. I gave Him my life, my money, my time and my family. I promised Him that with His help I would solve my financial problems and most of all I would put my almost broken marriage back together.

I was late getting downstairs, but that didn't really matter to me. I was on top of the world and couldn't care less.

I could not wait to get home and surprise Gina with what had happened to me. We sat at the table and Gina laughed and cried and when I had calmed down, she said "I've got to tell you how sweet the Lord is and how fast He can work if you are sincere in your prayers and it is His will to answer them."

"When I went upstairs for bed last night I got on my knees and asked the Lord to make you read and study the Bible and if you weren't really saved to show you how to be saved. What time did you go upstairs and begin to pray, Honey?" I turned off the television when the 11:00PM news came on, so It was right after 11:00PM when I began praying."

Now if you want to see how fast God can answer a prayer, I invite you to go back to my first paragraph in this chapter and see what time our conversation about the Bible and being saved took place and you'll see why Joe's question didn't go with my comment. That wasn't Joe talking, that was my Lord and my Savior taking action on Gina's prayer.

Psalm 55:14. "We took sweet counsel together and walked unto the House of God in company."

HAPPINESS

Happiness, happiness – Oh shy eluder!

I reach out to touch thy golden face,

But grasp vacuums of emptiness.

Can't I ever discover thy hiding Place?

Happiness, happiness – Oh, prankish elf!

Dare I hope to find thy secret treasure.

Years of endless searching leave me

Longing to fill my void with pleasure.

Happiness, happiness –Oh, frisky sea!

I set my sails to find thy shore

I groom my ship and chart my coarse,

Only to learn I'm shipwrecked once more.

Happiness, happiness –Oh, beautiful joy!

Art thy a gift or hard-earned metal?

To help another hungry soul.

Strangely brings the peace to calm and settle

Happiness, happiness – Oh prize from above.

Thank God my hopeless search is ended

For thou cannot be grabbed or bought

But only in Christ are broken hearts mended.

    Gina Greene

CHAPTER XVIII
THE BURGER KING

I Peter 2:2, "As newborn babes, desire the sincere milk of the word, that ye may grow thereby:"

O.J. and I were like a couple of kids on Christmas morning. We were so excited and happy we were dancing and singing all the time. Something new has happening too, we were hugging and kissing all the time. It was marvelous!

As I began to examine my life and all the events that had led up to the salvation of my husband, I could see a pattern that was very similar to the wanderings of the Children of Israel.

I had left Egypt my old sin-filled nature at an early age of 15, then I headed out eagerly to find my Utopia that flowed with milk and honey. Somehow, I lost sight of that promised land and began to grumble with the way things were going for me on the wilderness trip. God had to send me off on some by-passes in order to bring me back to the place that He wanted me to be. I wore the same old sandals of sin and rags of helplessness as I marched around in circles for ten long years.

Finally one glorious day I mustered up the courage to cross over Jordan into the promised land. This was the day I finally surrendered my will to God and said- "I don't know what I'll find on the other side, but it has to be better than what I now know. When I crossed over Jordan, I thought the victory was won, but it was only the beginning. I didn't really understand when the Lord said..."Sanctify yourselves for tomorrow the Lord will do wonders among you." Jeremiah 3:5

I had expected everything to be beautiful and eat my fill of the Lord's blessings, but there was still one major battle that had to be won before I could actually possess this new land. No sooner had I taken my last step out of the river than I looked up to face the walls of the City of Jericho. Boy, were there giants in that place! I was about to run again, when the Lord spoke to my heart and said, "I've already given you the victory, but you have to march out in faith to claim the city!"

Wow! That was an overwhelming task for me! The battle lasted for three very long months. Finally after agonizing days of marching and waiting the Lord said, "Shout, for the Lord hath given you the city," Jeremiah 6:16. I trusted God and after the walls of Jericho fell, out of the rubble came my husband's salvation. Oh Victory of Victories!

One important lesson I had learned, it was not ever going to be "easy" to be a Christian. But it was going to be wonderful working along with my brand new husband, slowly building up a solid Christian foundation and home for our children. No, it wasn't all instantly worked out and we did not live like I had always imagined we would – like they do in the "and they lived happily ever after" fairy tales, But it was a "beautiful" beginning.

O.J. was bursting with joy. He wanted to call all our friends and tell them that he had finally found Christ. We decided to call Lee and Barb one night about 3:00am. As soon as Lee realized it was O.J., he asked, "O.J. are you drunk?"

We both felt a little drunk and crazy and as if we might just fly away with joy! We had been carrying heavy burdens for so long and now – it was as if someone had set us free. We would sit and talk about the Lord for hours at the time. When our friends would drop by we would almost fight for an opportunity to tell them about what was happening in our lives. There are no words to describe the depth of our feelings and the love that was beginning to grow in our hearts for each other.

We decided that we had found a good church and should become active in it. Forrest Hills had a large bus ministry and we took a route and in one month we built it from 7 to 53 riders.

O.J. began to realize during the next few weeks that he needed to be baptized. He admitted to me that he felt a little embarrassed to be baptized since he had already been immersed twice. I assured him that no one in this church would know that, so he decided to go ahead. While he was preparing to come out into the pool for his baptism, John Reynolds, the Associate Pastor was introducing everyone and said, "I know O.J. won't mind me telling this, but this is the "third" time he has been baptized." Of course, by this time O.J. didn't mind and actually this was the first time he had been baptized since he had not been a Christian before.

We were on the mountain top and it was marvelous! Everyone warned us that we would have to come down sooner or later, but not us – we just knew this was the way it would be forever! We had been so miserable that we had earned this Utopia ! But as you already know, nothing stays perfect, not even with the best intentions.

After O.J. had been saved for about one month he began feeling the Lord would have him go out on church visitation. Lee and Barbara Baugh had stopped in on their way across the States to visit us for a few days and Lee decided that he would go with O.J. this Thursday night on visitation.

We were all sitting around the kitchen table having hamburgers for dinner. For some reason O.J. had gotten in one of his griping moods, much the same as he would do before he had trusted Christ. I was trying to be patient, but my nerves were really on edge. "And wipe that ketchup off your face!" were the fatal words for O.J. because that was the straw that broke "my" back. Before I even realized what I was doing I had flung my hamburger right into O.J.'s face. I always put a lot of ketchup on my burger and this hamburger was no exception – so- down his face and onto his clean dress shirt and on down onto his pants rolled the bun, meat and especially the KETCHUP!

O.J. was speechless and his face showed no expression whatsoever! I was Horrified! I couldn't believe that I had thrown that hamburger and no one else at the table could believe it either.

O.J. slowly got up, wiped his face and walked upstairs to change clothes. "Lord, I've really blown it now. Here he was about to go out on his first visitation night and I have to do this! I'm crazy! He may walk out and never come back, Lord. Please let him forgive me even before I ask him and let him come on back down stairs."

My prayers were interrupted with the doorbell ringing. It was Dwight Long, one of the men from church who was picking up O.J. and Lee. "What in the world will I tell him? Now everyone will know about the problems we have had in the past and now we have problems again! Lord, please help me out of this mess!" About that time O.J. came down the stairs and KISSED me good-bye! I whispered in his ear, " please forgive me." He squeezed my hand and walked out the door. I knew then I truly had a "New Honey."

Philippians 3:13-14, "Brethren, I count not myself to have apprehended; but this one thing I do, forgetting those things which are behind, and reaching forth unto those things which are before. I press toward the mark for the prize for the high calling of God in Christ Jesus."

CHAPTER XIX
QUIET VICTORY

James 1:3-4, "Knowing this, that the trying of your faith worketh patience...But let patience have her perfect work, that ye may be perfect and entire, wanting nothing.

I was beginning to think I was about one step away from being perfect because I didn't think my faith could have been tried anymore! I came to realize that I had a personal devil, just as I had a personal Savior. He just couldn't stand for me and O.J. to be happy, and especially happy in the Lord. Since he couldn't attack our marriage anymore he began to hit us in other ways. Oh, they were sly at first, but soon his attacks became more and more bolder.

O.J. told our Bus Pastor, Johnny Stancil, that he felt God was calling us to work in the Bus Ministry, but he knew he would have to be away some of the time on weekends. That meant it would be up to me to decide if I could handle it alone on those times. I was so thrilled that I jumped at the opportunity to do something for my Lord.

"Why, I'll just ask the Lord to let you be home on weekends, that should be simple enough for the God who parted the Red Sea." But, it didn't work out exactly the way I had planned, the Lord had some lessons for me to learn. O.J. was gone for SIX weeks after we surrendered to take the bus route. I was so mad at the devil that one Saturday, I yelled at him saying, "You can keep O.J. away for SIX MONTHS, but I am going to carry this bus route on". So the next morning I woke up with pneumonia.

When O.J. finally was home Saturday to visit the route and on Sunday to drive the bus we really felt the presence of the Lord. There was only a handful of kids when we took the route over and soon we had over 75 regulars. I remember one Sunday particularly.

We had promised to take the kids to Lion Country Safari after church, so they all brought their friends. We had about 115 kids on that old church bus. It was the middle of August and I was pregnant. I know the temperature must have been at least 110 degrees on that bus.

The gate keeper told us not to let any of the windows down because of the lions reaching in, so – there we were, 115 hot screaming kids and a big fat mama! It was a long drive thru the park and the kids had already been in church all morning, so we all needed to use the rest room – which there was not one to be found, even if we could get off the bus. I was beginning to doubt if it was the Lord's will for any of us to be out there and even if I was sane! But on the way home one of the little boys came and sat down beside me and told me that he had asked Christ to come in his heart in Sunday School that morning, and he was so happy that I knew it was worth every bit of the hassle.

Not long after that, the Lord blessed us with our third baby, a beautiful little girl that we named Jennifer Elaine. She is very special because she was the last and the one that O.J. prayed with me about before she was born. I can truly thank the Lord now that we did not have the babies that I lost due to miscarriage, because they would have been old enough to know their Daddy before he was saved. But, he was saved one month before our first daughter, Tiffany Koren, ~~who~~ was saved at age four, and she cannot remember what it was like before that time. The Lord is so merciful!

I had to stop riding the bus on Sunday morning after Jeni was born to care for her, but my heart remained with those precious boys and girls that O.J. drove to Sunday School every Sunday morning. They called him Mr. O.J. and me Miss O.J. Many of them came to know Christ as a result of our visiting them, handing out bubble gum and loving them.

One Sunday we had a guest speaker to bring the morning message. It was a Missionary, and the moment I head the verse that was the text of the message my heart leaped! Isaiah 6:8, "Also I heard the voice of the Lord, saying whom shall I send and who will go for us? Then said I, Here am I: send me." I had almost forgotten the commitment I had made to the Lord on this verse. What in the world was I to do now? I couldn't possibly go to the mission field now, I had a husband and three children.

O.J. was saved and loved the Lord, but he felt no call to the mission field and he would think me crazy if I told him about the call I had felt. I was afraid to tell the Lord that I was willing to go now because I was afraid He might take my family away from me. What, oh what, was I to do? I couldn't fight back the tears any longer when Lynn Long came up to me and asked me what was the matter. "I'll call you and explain later," I quickly told her. I just couldn't bring myself to tell O.J. and I was afraid he might overhear.

I didn't call her for a few days, I was going through agony trying to figure out what I could do. When I did call, she was very sweet and understanding and offered to pray for me. I knew I needed some good counsel about what to do, but I just was so scared and stubborn that I refused help from anyone.

I stayed in this state for two weeks, until I could bear it no longer and told the Lord I was willing to do whatever He wanted from me, no matter what the cost. It was not until that moment that I realized He would not demand any such horrible price as I had feared, but instead wanted my happiness much more than I did.

He spoke so tenderly to my heart and said, "I need missionaries at home too." (Thank the Lord for plan B) "Yes, Lord, yes, yes, I promise I will be that missionary for You. I know that is one thing I can do. I can raise my children according to your word and share with other wives the lessons you have taught me. I promise to do that!" It was then that I was able to tell O.J. about the private hell that I had been going through and he just laughed and said "Silly," as only he can. I knew that he truly did understand and that we both would be missionaries for the Lord at home.

CHAPTER XX
FACES IN THE WINDOW

Romans 5:20"…Where sin abounded, grace did much more abound."

Have you ever had the feeling that someone was watching you even though you could not see him? That was exactly the feeling I had as we were moving into our new dream home. It was all the things we had ever hoped for, rolled into one.

It was a beautiful balanced wing, French style house with huge rooms, an intercom that played soft music everywhere, and a beautiful chandelier that hung all the way down from the second floor into the entrance hall. As you sat at the breakfast table you looked out onto a lovely, heated pool surrounded by a large terrace. Beyond that lay rolling green pastures and a stable for our horses. We thought the Lord had given this splendid home to us for the rest of our lives, and we had every intention of using it for His glory.

For some reason, however, we could not seem to get settled in this new environment. There was so much confusion and many unusual problems. I kept saying to myself, "You have just had a baby three months ago, and it's going to take you a while to feel like yourself again. Soon you will be straightened out." But, that day never seemed to come. After living in the house for about three weeks

I began to realize something very strange was going on. Still I tried to dismiss each mysterious incident with the idea that I was tired and simply letting my imagination run away with me.

Late one Monday night ~~with~~ my sister, Elaine, and my brother, Ralph, were visiting me and we were all sitting in the kitchen discussing God's word. As we talked we began to argue about some of the characters of the Bible—as to whether Jonah was dead when the whale swallowed him and whether Paul was dead when he was stoned and saw the wonders of Heaven.

It seemed like a very valid argument until our conversation was interrupted with three very loud KNOCKS! My first thoughts were that someone was at the front door, but it seemed odd that the dogs were not barking. We all felt a little uneasy, so it was decided that we would take a look together. We went to every door and window and could see nothing.

Count, our faithful German Shepherd of thirteen years, was acting very curious. We walked with him through every room, checked under every bed and in every closet. The only noise to be heard now was the hall clock as it rang out ten long times. The whole house echoed with silence, but still there was a definite awareness of a foreign presence. Yet we found no one!

"It must be that the Lord has sent an angel down to remind us that we do not argue about His Word." I said. "Let's pray and ask the Lord to forgive us." Elaine and Ralph agreed that that sounded like a great idea!

Sleep did not come very easy that night, but I upheld the idea that I was just imagining things. Still problems continued to develop. All the faucets in the house had stopped working. We could not even take a shower. My old faithful vacuum cleaner exploded and left me with a dreadful mess. Next, the oven decided not to bake the cake I had planned as a surprise for my husband. "Won't O.J. ever come home?" I began to think. As O.J. walked in the door I knew something was wrong. The car had broken down and left him stranded. "How much more could happen?" I began to question, "Had the Lord really given us this "dream" home?"

Another week of nightmares slowly passed and finally it was Monday night again. The entire family had spent most of the day bickering about petty things, things that Christ had long since removed from our midst. It seemed that we were constantly at each other's throats. Everything the children did annoyed me, and I found it very difficult to hold back my temper. Even O.J. and I were beginning to pick at and complain to each other—something we had not done since he had become a Christian. What in the world was happening to us?

O.J. left to go out on a flight about 4:00 that afternoon and I was so exhausted I lay down for a nap. I simply could not understand why I never seemed to find the time to get things in order around the house. I was always tired and those old feelings of depression were troubling me more and more these days.

After dinner Elaine and Ralph joined me again and we sat talking in the kitchen as we so often did. This time we agreed not to argue about anything, especially the Bible. Instead we began to praise the Lord and talk about His goodness to us. We each took turns quoting favorite verses and sharing how they had been a particular blessing to us. Suddenly, all the talking was interrupted by those same three thundering KNOCKS! It was the kind of noise that made you stop whatever you were doing or saying and just listen. It made the hair stand up on my head and chill bumps run all up and down my body. I KNEW this time that those knocks were not of the Lord!

The verse II Timothy 1:7, "For God hath not given us the spirit of fear; but of power, and of love, and of a sound mind," kept going over and over in my head. I did not even bother to go to see if there was anyone at the door. It seemed as if the knocks had come over the intercom system and centered in the laundry room. They were very slow, deliberate knocks. KNOCK! KNOCK! KNOCK! Fear such I have never known began to grip my whole being. "Elaine, is it possible for Satan to inhabit houses?" I knew there was someone with us that was not of the Lord whom we served. The sweet Holy Spirit in my heart did not bear witness with this spirit. It was foreign to everything in me.

Somehow I never had visualized Satan as a real person just as Jesus Christ is a real person. I saw Satan as some kind of vague spirit floating around only affecting drunks and people engaged in horrible sin. How very wrong I was! And how Satan loved this delusion he had created! I had thought after O.J. was saved that everything was going to be wonderful and easy from now on, kind of like the fairy tales that end with "and they lived happily ever after." Nothing could have been farther from the truth.

"We can't just sit here, we have to do something," Ralph said. But what? Terror clutched our hearts. We were literally frozen in horror. Once more the long silence was broken as the hall clock struck 10:00. This was no coincidence, it was only one week ago that we had sat in exactly the same place at exactly the same time and heard and felt this grotesque presence.

"We've got to pray," I whispered. We began praying, not daring to close our eyes, asking for the Divine protection of our Heavenly Father. Together we read Psalm 91: "He that dwelleth in the secret place of the most High shall abide under the shadow of the Almighty…thou shalt not be afraid for the terror by night; nor for the pestilence that walketh in darkness;… There shall no evil befall Thee, neither shall any plague come nigh thy dwelling. For He shall give His angels charge over Thee, to keep thee in all thy ways."

We continued to claim God's promises and to pray until 2:00a.m. Weary from the battle we decided to go to bed and try to get some sleep. Over and over I quoted "Greater is He that is in you than he that is in the world." (I John 4:4) I knew I had Christ's presence to protect me, but I also knew that this evil force would return to frighten and torment me.

O.J. returned home the next morning at 6:00a.m. I really don't know exactly what had happened to make him aware of all the weird things that were going on, but somehow when he walked in the door, he realized what was happening. We had never talked about it. I never believed in ghosts, or spooks, or whatever people ordinarily call them, and neither did my husband. We always imagined ourselves to be normal, rational people and they don't talk about "Spirits." But, now there was no escaping the fact that something "out of the ordinary" was taking place in our home.

I had finally fallen asleep from sheer exhaustion and O.J. hated to wake me, so he quietly lay down beside me and began to pray. He had never had any experience with "Evil Spirits" and certainly did not know what to say, neither did he have any magic formula to rid our home of their foreboding intrusion, but the Lord's Grace is always sufficient.

Slowly he began commanding Satan to leave in the Blessed Name of our Lord and Savior Jesus Christ. Time seemed to stand still, and even now he can't recall how long he must have prayed, but at last he heard a loud THUMP in the attic, similar to the sound of a large book turning over. O.J. continued to pray. All at once pain began to pierce his body; it was as if he were in a very cold shower in which the drops of water felt like cold needles. He knew the only thing left to do now was to pray and hang onto the Lord, so pray he did! After what seemed like and eternity, the window positioned right in front of our bed began to shake and made a loud noise. Suddenly, everything was quiet and O.J. began to feel the warming assurance of the Holy Spirit once more.

At the breakfast table the next morning there was a quiet calm that we had never felt in that house before. We all knew that we had to talk about the events of the night before and yet everyone was afraid that the other might think them insane. There was a closeness in the family that had been missing for weeks.

One by one we began to relate experiences that had taken place over the entire stay in our new and very strange domain. I had not dared to mention that each time I went into the hall bath and looked into the mirror, I would see from the corner of my eye someone standing in the hall. When I would turn, he would always disappear. I couldn't recall the number of times I would see a face peering in through one of the windows, always to find it vanished upon close examination. Elaine admitted to the time she walked into her dark room and spoke to O.J. thinking he was standing there in the dark only to find an empty room as soon as she turned on the light. It was such a feeling of relief to discover I was not hallucinating or at best losing control of my senses.

By this time, every electrical appliance in the entire house was broken, some of which had to be fixed several times. When I went into the laundry room later that morning to do the wash, I found the tub completely picked up out of the washer, sitting to one side. The intercom refused to work at all. Garbage was strewn all over the garage and yard from dogs who had paid us a visit. There was utter and complete confusion in every room. The entire place bore the marks of our most unwelcome guests.

In the weeks and months that lay ahead our problems diminished, but they did not entirely disappear. Jennifer, my youngest child, became ill with a serious ear infection. Despite all efforts made by the doctor and large doses of antibiotics she continued to have a low grade fever. It was decided that surgery was the only answer, however, they could not operate until her temperature returned to normal.

I prayed and prayed for her to be healed, but still there was no change. One day while reading my Bible, I came across the verses, James 5:14&15 "Is any sick among you? Let him call for the elders of the church: and let them pray over him, anointing him with oil in the name of the Lord: And the prayer of faith shall save the sick, and the Lord shall raise him up; ..." It seemed the Lord was speaking to me with these passages and I knew what I had to do.

I spoke with my pastor about it, afraid of his reaction, but found him to be very concerned and willing to help. The morning I was to bring Jenny [Jeni] into his office, it was raining and was so cold I was afraid to take her out, but I had trusted God when He said in His word that the prayer of faith would heal the sick, and that was what I was holding on to. Dr. Curtis Hutson is a very busy man, but as we approached his office he invited us right in. He tenderly took hold of Jenny's [Jeni's] hand and began to pray and ask for God's healing. He did not ask for any overnight miracle, but that upon Jenn's [Jeni's] next visit, the doctor would see that a miracle had taken place.

As I drove home that day I knew God was going to heal Jenny [Jeni], there was never any doubt in my mind, but I also knew that something was causing this terrible oppression. O.J. and I discussed over and over what each of us thought might be the problem. Then together we realized that what we must do was claim every inch of our house and land for the Lord. It had been Satan's territory for too long and he was reluctant to give it up. After parking in the car and carefully tucking the children in bed, O.J. and I held hands and walked around the entire property proclaiming this area to be the Lord's. An indescribable peace came into our home that day as we remembered God's promise in John 16:33, "These things I have spoken unto you, that in Me ye might have peace. In the world ye shall have tribulation; but be of good cheer; I have overcome the world."

Two weeks went by and it was time for us to go in for Jeni's check-up. I was so impatient to hear what the diagnosis would be that I could hardly wait for the doctor to finish his examination. "Something more that medicine has done this," was his first comment. "Someone has been praying for this child." God had not only healed Jeni, but had also answered Dr. Hutson's prayer. Since my pediatrician is a Christian we had a wonderful time praising God that day.

When I returned home, I knew that God had at long last gotten the victory in our house and that Satan would no longer be a constant intruder. Oh yes, I knew that He would always pace to and fro seeking to devour me, but no longer would he be the conqueror. For Christmas that year, Elaine gave us a handsome plaque that contained the verse we had chosen as our own. Romans 5:20 …"Where sin abounded, grace did much more abound." We hung it above the front door as a constant reminder that the house had been fought for, conquered, and claimed for the Lord.

CHAPTER XXI
GREENE ACRES

Philippians 4:11 "Not that I speak in respect of want; for I have learned in whatsoever state I am, therewith to be content."

"Your life is a CIRCUS!" Barbara had come to stay with us for a few days to rest and recover from the hassle of speaking and touring around the country and now she was telling me that my life was more hectic that the one she was supposed to be recovering from. I had never thought about it before. I suppose I just accepted all the unusual things that happened to us all the time as "normal". Only very good friends can tell you the truth and not make you angry, and Barbara was such a friend.

As she was trying to tell us how we must slow down, we were interrupted by the phone ringing. It was a lady who was in a desperate situation. Her husband was drinking and had been pushing her around again. She was a Christian and he resented that.

My heart went out to her as I tried to encourage her in the lessons I had learned before O.J. trusted Christ. I knew that the Lord had called me to exhort other ladies in their faith in Christ. It was hard to slow down and tell these ladies when they called that I was busy with my family and could not talk. As a result, my phone rang day and night.

"Come on out and help me feed the animals", I invited Barb to join me in my daily chores as keeper of the zoo that we had managed to collect over the years. As we walked out to the barn we were followed by our four dogs, the leader of whom was Count, our old faithful German Shepherd of thirteen years, nipping at his heels, his son, a young pup we called Rudy, a collie named Ladd, who could roll up his lip and smile at you, and a toy poodle named Fifi who was totally useless.

At the barn we were met by our three horses, Daisy Mae, Tiffany's mare that she rides in local horse shows, her new colt Shaddrack, and a little brown pony named Dolly. They all ran up to the barn and into their stalls waiting to be fed, while the chickens came scratching around hoping some of the grain would drop and they would be the first to find it.

All this commotion caused our old cat, a Siamese named Dutch, to jump from his position in the hay loft where he had been searching for some mice. "Elmer", the head rooster, seemed to resent the intrusion and came running at us with his feathers standing straight up! I hated this rooster! He was a black game chicken that I had accidently gotten in with some hens that I had ordered through the mail. But, I didn't have the heart to eat him, so I tolerated his insults and ran when he came toward me.

By the time we got back up to the house we were both out of breath and I just wanted to go to bed. But I still had the three hamsters

119

and two aquariums full of fish to feed for the night, plus the dinner dishes to wash and the kids to bathe and on and on and on. Yes, I suppose our life is a circus. Sometimes I just want to sit down forever and do nothing, but I supposed I would be bored. This is the life the Lord has given us, and He knows best. There are times, however, when I wonder what the Lord is teaching us. I remember questioning our life style the day that Daisy spooked as the pony Trey was on ran up behind her. Daisy kicked out to hit the pony and got Trey's leg instead. It all happened so fast that no one knew exactly what had occurred.

Trey cried, but only for a few minutes, so we didn't dream that his leg was broken. However, we decided to take him to the hospital and have it x-rayed just to be sure. We were shocked when the doctor came out and told us that his leg was fractured just below the knee. He was in a cast for six weeks and had to miss the rest of that year in kindergarten.

After the second year at Greene Acres I began to think there must be a better way to spend the summers than bathing and clipping a horse. However, Tiffany insisted that Daisy must be groomed perfectly for her horse shows, and O.J. always seemed to be away on a trip when the day for Daisy to be groomed came around.

Bleaching a horse's tail just is not a pleasant way to spend an afternoon! But when I would see Tiffany riding in that ring, sitting so tall in that saddle, I knew it was worth it. She learned many valuable lessons that many adults never learn throughout their entire lives.

One horse show in particular stands out in my mind. She had won ribbons in all the previous shows in which she had competed, so this Saturday she was confident that she would place at least second or third. She really had not worked Daisy as much as she should, and neither Tiffany nor her horse was prepared for the show. However, Tiffany rode her into the ring proudly and very confidently. As the judge began calling out the winners, we waited to hear him call out her number, but he named first, second, third, fourth, and now there were only two people left in the ring, Tiffany and one other little girl. As he called out the fifth place winner, the other girl rode up to accept the ribbon leaving Tiffany as the only person in the ring. I'll never forget the look on her face as she slowly rode from the stadium trying to fight back the tears.

"Why didn't I win, Mommy?" she pleaded with me to tell her. "I prayed and asked the Lord to please let me win at least fifth place. Why didn't he answer my prayer?" My heart was breaking for her. "I don't know, Honey," I told her. "I was praying, too. I'm truly sorry."

We didn't say anything else as we walked back to the stalls where we would unsaddle Daisy and load her back in the trailer to go home. It had been a horribly disappointing day, and no one could find any words that seemed sufficient.

As we rode along in the car on the way home, suddenly Tiffany blurted out, "I know why I didn't win today!" "You do?" O.J. and I both asked at the same time. "Yes. My teacher taught us the verse last week in Galatians 6:7 that says, 'Be not deceived; God is not mocked;

for whatsoever a man soweth, that shall he also reap.' I didn't practice and work Daisy for the show, and God couldn't let me win."

She had learned a precious lesson and one that she would never forget. She was even able to apply this to her work in school as she would study and prepare for tests. Praise God for the simple and painful lesson He taught all of us through this last horse show.

As soon as we arrived at home it was back to the usual routine of feeding the animals and trying to calm Daisy down after the excitement of the horse show. While we were outside putting the trailer away and settling everything down for the night, the phone rang.

It was decided that I would be the one to run to answer it, since it was probably for me anyway. Sure enough, it was Susan, a dear friend that I had been counseling for about a year. She was calling long distance and needed some reassuring words. While I was trying to find just the right things that the Lord would have me share with her, the back door opened and in came the whole family, shouting something about her <u>leg</u> being broken. "Whose leg?" I was almost afraid to ask.

Just then I looked around the corner and there stood O.J. in the middle of my kitchen with a CHICKEN in his arms! He was looking for a bandage. "What are you doing with that CHICKEN in my kitchen?" I yelled at him, forgetting all about Susan on the other end of the phone. "I was trying to get her down off the rafters so I could shut all the chickens up for the night, and her leg just snapped!", he admitted with such guilt and compassion that I was really surprised. "Can't you fix some sort of splint for her leg?"

Suddenly, I remembered Susan on the phone. "Oh my, this is long distance, Honey. Just a minute and I'll see what I can do." "Sue, forgive me, but I'll have to call you back. You see one of our chickens just broke her leg and…" "That's what I thought I heard," Susan answered with the sound of total disbelief in her voice. Then she added "Gina, I love you. Call you later, O.K.?" "Sure, Sue, you call me anytime."

We took two popsicle sticks and some white tape and bandaged the broken leg as the hen looked up at us almost as if to say, "what in the world are you nuts doing?" Trust me, I was thinking the same thing.

Count walked with us as we carried the chicken back to the barn and O.J. tenderly placed her on the nest. Count was our overseer and protector. Nothing happened at the Greene Acres without his knowing about it.

He was the "king" and all the other animals made room for him. He ate first and chose where he would lay down. Then the others would follow suit. We noticed that night that he seemed weak and could not get around as easily as before.

As the weeks passed, Count became slower and slower and before long he could hardly get around at all. He was thirteen years old, and that was terribly old for a German Shepherd. Finally one day, he could get up no longer and we had to say good-bye to him. Count became a part of our family when he was four days old and I could hold him in the palm of my hand. Now I thought my heart would break as we stood before his grave out behind the old barn.

"Good bye dear, faithful friend." He would lick my tears when I cried and run with me what I was happy. Now his body was still and he would share those days with me no longer. The children asked me, "Will Count be in Heaven when we get there?" That has always been a tough question for parents, but I remembered something I had read and I shared that with them. "Someone once said that if having Count or any other pet with you in Heaven is necessary for you to be happy, then I'm sure he will be."

As we held hands and walked back up to the house, I thanked the Lord for all the years He had allowed us to love and enjoy Count. Then I thanked the Lord for the other animals and the joy they would continue to bring us. I suppose losing Count made us appreciate all the other animals we had at Greene Acres.

Yes, we do live in a zoo and our life is a circus, but I'm thankful for our home. I'm thankful that it is a busy, exciting, loving, happy place, and one thing for sure—it's never boring!

CHAPTER XXII
I BELIEVE IN MIRACLES!

Psalm 43:5, "Why art thou cast down, O my soul? And why art thou disquieted within me: Hope in God: for I shall yet praise Him, who is the health of my countenance and my God."

"I feel a lump in your left breast, Mrs. Greene," the doctor told me as I was laying on the examination table undergoing my annual physical. "Would you please say that one more time?" I asked. I simply could not believe that I had heard him correctly. "There is a small lump in your left breast, and I want a surgeon to take a look at it. As soon as you are dressed, step into my office, I want to talk with you about it." I was so stunned that I really couldn't react. I mechanically reached for my clothes and somehow managed to get them on. It was such a shock! I had never felt better in my life. In fact, I had nearly cancelled my appointment because it seemed silly to waste so much time, however, O.J. had convinced me that I should have a check-up.

The doctor was writing on my chart as I entered his office. "Sit down. I can't tell for sure what this lump might be, so I want this surgeon to examine it," he said, as he handed me a card. "Now, I want you to follow his advice whatever it may be." What in the world did he mean, "WHATEVER, it may be?"

Of course, by this time I could only think the worse. Doctors don't ask you to see a surgeon if it's not serious. "Go out and walk and collect your thoughts," was his advice. My doctor was not a Christian and I knew how important my reaction to this "shock" was. I managed to mumble some words that the Lord knew best and quickly slipped out. I knew I had to cry or scream or something and I could not let this man see me!

As I stepped into the hall I was thankful to find it empty. "Lord, please don't let anyone be on the elevator with me." I just had to be alone. I had to think and somehow comprehend what the doctor had meant. Thoughts were whirling through my mind and at the same time I felt void of all emotion.

"Why can't I cry? I must be dreaming. This CANNOT be real. I've been through so much in the past. Now we are living for God and He wouldn't allow anything like this to happen to me." Still I knew that I had to face reality and suddenly I realized that I had to tell my family. What would their reaction be? I had left the children with Mother and it was strange to remember her last words as I walked out the door. I had said that I could see no reason for this check-up because I felt great. "Sometimes that's when you really NEED to see a doctor," Mother cautioned. What would she think now when she learned that she had been so right?

I drove as slowly as I possibly could. I knew that O.J. would be busy in the yard or in the garden and I wondered how I would go about telling him. If I did have to have surgery, would he still love me? We had both become so busy over the last few weeks that we had begun to drift apart. It seemed that there were never enough hours in the day, the phone never stopped ringing with people who had problems and just wanted someone to listen, then the house and garden were a full time job not to mention three demanding children. I had felt so stretched that I had prayed and asked God to give me some relief. Was this some strange answer to my prayer?

I remembered just one week ago, some dear friends had come to visit us for a few days and Barbara had said, "Gina, this is a ZOO! I don't see how you stand it!" Lee had been very concerned about O.J. because he worked without any let up. If he was not out on a trip, then he was cutting the yard, which was over an acre, or cleaning the pool or repairing some damage that had been done by the horses or children. We couldn't eat a meal together without taking the phone off the hook and refusing to answer the door. "Boy, things will certainly come to a standstill now!" I thought.

As I pulled into the garage I could see that I had been right, O.J. was on his tractor in the pasture. I got out of the car and began to walk very slowly out to where he was working. Still I had no idea of how I would tell him. "He'll probably ask me to wait until dinner, so that he can finish what he is doing," I thought. But I could hear the tractor stop and O.J. was getting off. He began to walk very fast toward me. "What's wrong?" he called out! I could not believe it.

I didn't have to try to find the right words at all; he already knew that something had happened. I could hold back the tears no longer. "The doctor found a lump in my breast!" Those were the only words I could manage to get out. "Come out here and let's pray," he said. We sat down on an old stump and O.J. began to thank the Lord for all His blessings and to ask Him to heal my body. What had I been so afraid of? I have never felt the presence of the Lord as real, and have never felt the love of my husband as certain. A peace came into my heart and I too began to thank God for whatever would come.

Telling my parents and O.J.'s parents would not be so easy. At first we thought it might be best to wait until I had seen the surgeon, but I felt that they had a right to know and I desperately needed their support and prayers. I had been gone so long that they had all begun to wonder what was wrong. It seemed that God had prepared each of their hearts for the news, because they received it so well. I know that they were frightened, just as I was, but they never allowed me to see that. They were so encouraging, never seeming to doubt for one minute that everything would be fine.

I knew the night would be the worst time. That's when Satan always hits me with worry and fear. I stayed up as late as possible, but eventually I knew I had to get some sleep. O.J. held me especially close that night. I never dreamed he could be so understanding. His behavior had really surprised me. I didn't know at the time, but my behavior had been even more of a surprise to him. Cancer was the thing that I feared most. It's strange that I was able to give the Lord my husband, my children, and every problem that was a real threat and yet this "possibility" was the one thing that I had held in reserve for my own private "worrying" sessions. I didn't realize that anyone else would see this in my life. But, now that I was face to face with the thing that I had thought I would never be able to face, it didn't seem as bad as I had imagined.

I knew the Lord would not allow anything to come into my life that would not be for my good and for the good of my family. I claimed the verse, "And He said unto me, my grace is sufficient for thee; for my strength is made perfect in weakness. Most gladly therefore, will I rather glory in my infirmities, that the power of Christ may rest upon me. Therefore, I take pleasure in infirmities, in reproaches, in necessities, in persecutions, in distresses for Christ's sake; for when I am weak, then am I strong." II Corinthians 12:9-10

I won't pretend that it was easy. Thoughts kept emerging like, "but what if?" and "Christians have to die too," but each time they did, I just quoted those scriptures over and over and finally I was actually able to thank the Lord for my problem. I knew for the first time what Ephesians 5:20 "Giving thanks ALWAYS for ALL things unto God and the Father in the name of the Lord Jesus Christ," really meant.

I called a few of my closest friends and asked them to pray for us. I was shocked at their attitude. They all said, "Oh, I know how afraid of cancer you are, I'll really pray for you." Now I knew why the Lord had caused me to have to face this. I was a terrible testimony for Him, I counseled ladies all day long and told them how to face and have victory over Satan and yet I had allowed him to conquer me in this area. This was one small closet I had left unopened to the Lord. I began to thank Him over and over for the opportunity to completely rely on Him and purposed that I would not leave one tiny speck in my life for Satan to reign over.

As the sun began to rise and peep into my bedroom window, I felt a peace and calm that said, "Fear not for I am with thee" Isaiah 43:5.

129

I phoned the surgeon as soon as his office opened. "You can come on in this afternoon, we have a cancellation," the nurse told me. I was so thankful; it was the waiting and not knowing that was so unbearable.

O.J. drove me to the office that afternoon and I never knew that ten miles could be so long. We rode in complete silence, holding hands and occasionally smiling at each other. As we walked into the office there were people sitting everywhere. I kept wondering if they were all facing serious problems in their lives. No one was talking, and no one dared look into anyone else's eyes. The silence was deafening!

The nurse finally called me back into the exam room. "Remove all your clothes and put this sheet over you," she told me. I always hate the ritual of seeing a doctor, but this was the worst yet! As I lay down on the table, I prayed it would not be too long before the doctor came in. The room was so cold, I began to shake. I guess I was shaking from nerves as much as the cold. The time dragged by, and I wanted to get up and run.

After what seemed an eternity, the door opened and an attractive, gray haired man walked into the room. "What seems to be your problem?" "My gynecologist found a lump in my left breast and said I should have you check it." My words would hardly come out. As he carefully checked each breast, he began to reassure me. "I don't believe it is too serious, but I am going to see if I can draw some fluid out of the lump."

I thought he would put me to sleep or at least give me some local anesthetic, but the nurse handed him a needle and suddenly BAM! He thrust the point into my breast as if he were giving me a shot.

When he drew it out, I could see no fluid. "Sometimes these lumps will disappear if you can draw the fluid out, I believe I saw a drop or two," he said.

"Now I want you to put hot compresses on this breast for two weeks and then come in. If this does not cause the lump to go away, then we will have to remove it." I could only think the worst again. But I knew I had to allow the Lord to have control of my mind, so I thanked him and said I would see him in two weeks, and I even managed a half smile.

O.J. looked relieved to see me walk out. As we drove home he said that he had been thinking and had decided that we needed to get away for a few days. That was one of the things I had been praying for before this entire nightmare happened. We both were so busy, that we had forgotten how to enjoy each other. I couldn't remember the last time we had carried on a conversation without at least four interruptions.

"Why don't you see if our folks will watch the children and we'll drive down to Jekyll Island for the weekend?" That sounded too good to be true! Three whole days ALONE! That was something we never did. I always felt guilty to leave the children, but now I knew that we both desperately needed this time together.

All sorts of weird thoughts ran through my head, but I kept them to myself. I knew that O.J. was worried too, but I could feel us drawing together in a new and deeper way. We had faced so many problems together in the fourteen years that we had been husband and wife, now this was a very different one and was bringing us even closer together. It was strange to be so uncertain and yet have so much peace in your heart. I could truly thank God for this problem because I could see His Hand in it even though I had no idea of the outcome.

Mother helped me do some shopping for the trip. I found a yellow jumpsuit that I knew was too expensive, but she convinced me that O.J. would like it, so I splurged and bought it. I felt a bit like a child again planning for such an exciting outing.

I had my hair trimmed and my nails manicured and I really felt like I was about to embark on an exciting adventure. Just as I was about to leave the shopping center, something caught my eye. There in the store window hung the loveliest nightgown I had ever seen. I let go of all my inhibitions and got it! I knew O.J. would be shocked, but I hoped it would be a pleasant surprise!

O.J. had the car washed and everything prepared just right for the drive. We both were like school kids again, planning and laughing and even being a little silly. Both my mother and his were happy to keep the children for us and the children were thrilled at the prospects of a visit with both sets of grandparents.

Everything was finally packed and we were ready to leave. As we settled down into the car, O.J. said, "Let's pray before we leave." "Oh, thank you Lord," I kept saying over and over. I never dreamed we would even have a relationship such as this in my wildest dreams! It was worth every tear and heartache and a thousand more, just to be here at this moment and to feel this wonderful peace and joy and excitement that was racing through my heart! My thoughts kept going back to the last trip we had taken alone to Jamaica. How very different this one was!

We talked so much on the way down that my jaws ached like they did just after O.J. came home from the war in Viet Nam. We were busy making plans for the future and neither of us dared mention the dark shadow that might possibly come over them.

As we approached the islands, I had forgotten how beautiful they are. The whole time we had lived on St. Simons Island I had never taken the time to really look at it. It was just another stop on my long and empty search. But today, I could see all the beauty that Eugenia Price had seen and described in such detail. In her books she calls them the "Golden Isles" and today I could see why.

As the wind blows the tall grass, it gave the whole place a look of glistening gold. The tall oaks lined the roads while the regal Spanish moss reached down to touch each car as it passed. How had I missed all this loveliness before?

As we crossed the bridge to Jekyll Island I could see a maze of color Flowers of all kinds were growing between the lanes and on the sides of the road. The whole place was alive with color. In the background you could hear the birds singing and the ocean waves as they gently beat against the glistening sand. "Thank you, Lord, for allowing me to see, and to feel, and to be a part of all this wonder."

"Where would you like to go for dinner," O.J. interrupted my thoughts. "I'm going to take you to all the places we could not afford to go when we lived here," he announced. "Whatever you say," I happily replied. "I am your most grateful companion." I truly felt as if I were dating my young handsome Prince Charming again, only this time he was all the wonderful things I could ever imagine and thank God for. At the end of the day, we would walk on the beach and whisper "sweet nothings" in the moonlight. I dreaded for the trip to end, but all too quickly the day came that we had to go back home and back to reality.

We were very quiet during the drive home. We both knew that in three days I would have to go back to the doctor and if that lump had not completely gone away, then I would have to have surgery.

The lump did not go away, and I prepared for the worst. I was anxious to find out what the doctor would say and at the same time dreaded what he would tell me. O.J. went with me again and waited nervously. As the doctor walked into the room, I felt the presence of the Lord and knew that I was ready for whatever he would tell me. "My soul, wait thou only upon God: for my expectation is from Him." Psalms 62:5

" This lump has changed in composition and I believe it is just a clogged nodule," he announced. "I believe it will go away in time, but it is absolutely nothing to be concerned about." " Do you mean to tell me that I don't have to have an operation"? I was almost afraid to ask for fear I had misunderstood him. "No," he replied. "I believe it will go away if we just leave it alone.

O.J. could tell from my face when I walked out that everything was all right. He beamed back at me and we both thanked God for His wonderful grace and goodness.

Psalms 30:2, "O Lord my God, I cried unto thee, and thou hast healed me."

WHY ME, O LORD?

Why me, O Lord? Is the question that I pose,

I never have the time to sit or dream or doze,

My life is one big hassle

For its with Satan that I wrestle

A worthy opponent and near victor is he,

He causes me to stumble and take my eyes off Thee.

Why me, O Lord? Again and again I ask

Then I grit my teeth and straighten my mask.

No one must know the turmoil I feel.

Or how deep the wounds I must needs conceal.

I'll smile and laugh and wear a disguise.

They'll not know where the problem lies.

Why me, O Lord? I hear myself say

Please give me grace for one more day.

I've learned not to pray for patience at all.

Cause He answers that one as soon as I call.

It's trials and troubles I seem to know best.

Till finally I see the light thru the test.

Why me, O Lord? I'm thankful today.

You chose me and blest me in this sweet way.

A life with no problems is empty and dull.

Like a ship with no sails, but only a hull,

Only through clouds can we view the bright sun.

And tears make sweeter the victories we've won.

Why me, O Lord? With true joy in my heart.

You called me and sent me and set me apart.

You gave me a job though rocky the road.

But you're always there to carry the load.

The bigger the battle, the greater the win.

Thank you for grace and sweet peace within.

    Gina Greene

CHAPTER XXIII
SIX WHITE SHIRTS

Colossians 3:23, " And whatsoever ye do, do it hastily as to the Lord, and not unto men."

How does one begin to write a book, especially when one is a wife, a mother of three very active children and keeper of the zoo? I can't explain it, I only know that I feel I will burst if I can't share what God has brought me through with the hope that someone else might be given the same victory we now know.

Trey, my blonde eight year old, who has his Daddy's smile, asked in shocked amazement at the dinner table tonight, "You are going to write a book, YOU are going to write a book?!" And again I shyly answered, "Yes."

When I first began this book I really thought I would write it in a couple of weeks. I knew everything I wanted to say because it was simply the story of my long search for fulfillment and happiness. However, I was in for the surprise of my life! I didn't realize I needed a few more lessons on living before I could share with anyone else how to find their happiness.

I've heard other writers say that they felt as though they had given birth to a baby when they had finished writing their book. I must tell you that having a baby was "easy" for me, compared to writing this book! Every time I would feel that I would be able to finish it, something would happen to stop me.

Our lives underwent tremendous changes during the year that I was attempting to write this book. All my security was pulled out from under me and I found myself clinging to the Lord, I stopped writing this book over and over again and said, "It's not worth it! Nothing is worth this"!"

But as I am closing these final pages I know it IS worth it. If I can communicate to someone else who might be as miserable as I was for the ten long years before O.J. trusted Christ, then it will have been worth every bitter moment.

God has given me a story over all the years of tenderly leading me to this day and I have to tell it. I had so many obstacles to overcome. I didn't see how I could possibly find the time to write a letter much less a book, plus I am the world's worst speller and my grammar would stop a second grader! I knew I was no author, and if God wanted me to be the instrument to tell this story, then He would have to do it through me.

So....slowly, painfully, I asked Him to help me remember those terribly sad and bruised years so that I could relate them. There were times I would get mad at O.J. all over again and other times that I loved him terribly.

At first O.J. was a little reluctant for me to write everything so frankly and openly, but he gave me his permission to tell it. However, he was surprised the first time he read what I was writing and asked, "You're not going to use MY REAL NAME, are you?" "How else can I tell it?" I asked. Finally after the initial shock wore off he agreed that we had to be as honest as possible or else it would be of no value to anyone else.

O.J. has been so sweet to help me while I have been endeavoring to write, but a few days ago he came home carrying under his arm two boxes of white shirts. "Can you cut the sleeves off these shirts for me today?" he asked smiling his most irresistible smile. "Don't tell me, They were on sale, right?"

I knew O.J. could never resist a sale and these were "half price"! His motto throughout life has been: "If a little of something is good, then a lot is better". So….in he came carrying six, new white LONG sleeved shirts. He had needed SHORT sleeved ones, but they were not on sale –so----

Now if there is truly any one thing that I detest – it's sewing. Although I said "alright, I'll do it", in my heart I resented O.J. demanding so much of my time that I could spend studying or writing my book. I hung them up in the closet and mumbled to myself about ALL that was expected of me. I HATED the thought of "twelve" sleeves to be cut off and hemmed and I decided they could wait until I had more time.

The following day I had to go to the bookstore to inquire about a book for a friend. Books and particularly MY BOOK was the only thought that consumed my mind twenty four hours a day. As soon as I walked into the shop, people began asking if I had finished writing my book. I was on cloud nine until someone lowered the boom! Have you heard about the new book that Marion West has written? It is at the ~~published~~ publisher now and the name of it is "NO Turning Back." 'NO TURNING BACK,' I couldn't believe my ears! Are you sure? That was the name of MY BOOK!

How could the Holy Spirit do this to me? I truly believed that God had given that title to ME! I screamed "NO!" and stomped my feet. I suppose everyone in the store must have thought I had lost my mind. I decided they must be wrong. I would go home and call her and find out for myself.

I had never met Marion and I was very nervous, but felt I must call her. There must be some reason for the Lord to bring us together like this. She too, was a housewife in Lilburn and had begun writing very much the same way I had. So here goes…Marion was so sweet and we truly did have much in common. "NO TURNING BACK" however , was the name of her book. Apparently, the Lord had another name for my book and I would just have to trust Him to give it to me.

I sat down and prayed and begged the Lord to give me peace about this. "Please give me some title that I can work from." 'NO TURNING BACK' had been the whole theme of my book and without that title I didn't know where to begin. Would I have to start all over again? The harder I thought and prayed, the more blank my mind became.

My mind drifted back to the shirts hanging in the closet that needed altering. I told myself I would be the obedient wife I knew I should be, and start to work on them. I must admit I still did not relish the thought of sewing them, but I did love the man who would wear them, and furthermore, I was doing it for the Lord.

As I was sewing, slowly my heart began singing, and finally my lips joined in to form a tune. I really wasn't even conscious of what I was singing until finally I heard myself. " I FOUND THE HAPPY SIDE OF LIFE."

I Found The Happy Side Of Life, with Jesus as my Savior. I found a way, rolling along, singing a song, every single passing day. "I FOUND THE HAPPY SIDE. That was it! The title for my book, "I FOUND THE HAPPY SIDE."

That really described the book and my own feelings even more than the title that I thought I had to use. God was saying to me, "See when you do the things that you SHOULD first, then I'll allow you to do the things you WANT to do also. (Luke 12:31, 'But rather seek ye first the Kingdom of God and all these things shall be added unto you.')"

Why is it always so hard for me to give up my rebellion without a fight? I always begin every venture with NO! I'm not, I'm not… Well, maybe I will…I'm so thankful I did!

Living is a learning process for me, and I believe if I ever stop learning, then God will take me home. Thank you Lord, for the lesson today and thank you for the six white shirts that I thought I would never get around to doing. Thank you for a husband that loves you and me, and thank you especially for the joy I feel in my heart all (most) of the time.

I wish I could say that everything is wonderful and I never have any more problems, but that would be a lie. As the Psalmist said in Psalm 17:15, "As for Me...I shall be satisfied when I awake with thy likeness." I can say that I am on top of the circumstances now more than I am under them. I do have a song in my heart and sometimes I am so happy I dance all over the kitchen and click my heels like a school girl.

Thank you, Lord, that I found this side of life, THE HAPPY SIDE!!

CHAPTER XXIV
A SONG IN MY HEART

Ephesians 5:19, "Speaking to yourselves in psalms and hymns and spiritual songs, singing and making melody in your heart to the Lord".

Tonight as I sit at my desk writing, I truly can say I have a song in my heart. The children are all asleep and my dear faithful husband is out listening to an old friend pour out his heart to him. It seems so strange to hear these friends are having such serious problems – the very same problems God led us through almost six years ago. Had anyone told me at that time that O.J. would be counseling some else's husband I would have laughed. But, praise God, tonight he IS! (I am so happy I want to shout, He is able! He is able!)

For so many years we would not share our story of what the Lord had done for us because we were ashamed of our miserable past. Then one day I found a book in the bookstore written by Joyce Landorf, HIS STUBBORN LOVE. As I read her story, my eyes filled with tears and I began to cry openly. Their marriage had been similar to ours and Christ had brought them through with amazing VICTORY! I knew that day, that if she had the courage to share this part of their lives, that I too must in some way find the same courage to tell others what we had been through. My hope was that this book might help others just as her book had helped me.

I began teaching a ladies Bible Study in the home of a dear friend. I had felt the Lord dealing with me for five years about teaching a Bible Study. I never felt the time was right until I was talking to a lady that I had just led to Christ. She had been raised in a Catholic Girls School and her parents were Mormons. She had asked my mother-in-law what it meant to be "born again" and Grandma brought her to me. I showed her from the Bible the story of the religious man named Nicodemus who came to Jesus and asked Him the same question. Then I read John 3:16 to her and told her all that a person has to do is to trust Christ in child-like faith. Salvation has nothing to do with religion or church denomination. "You mean that's all there is to do?" "How could I have missed it all these years?"

She was wonderfully saved and knew firsthand what it meant to truly be "born again." Now she was a new baby in Christ, and had so many questions, "Have you ever thought of teaching a course in this?" she asked me. "As a matter of fact I have," I answered, "but not right now. I have to wait for the right time." Then suddenly I thought, "When is the time ever going to be right"? The last of my children had gone to school this year and I was free every morning until 12:00. NOW was the time that someone really needed a Bible Study. So right then I told the Lord yes, and my new friend in Christ, yes, I will teach a Bible Study.

It was in this Bible Study that I first found the courage to share my real testimony. Oh yes, I had given the story of my conversion in church many times, but I had never shared all the problems that O.J. and I had undergone and the miraculous change that Christ had brought in our lives. It was very painful at first-remembering – but many of the ladies came up to me and said "I am going through the same thing with my husband. Thank you for giving me hope." I knew then that I HAD to share my story.

The children can't remember what it was like before their Daddy was saved and I'm so thankful. I pray that they will be able to accept it when they learn the truth about our miserable past. I give that to Christ and know that He will provide when the time comes. I had tried to protect them by never allowing the full truth to come out, but I know now that I cannot and should not. When they are old enough I know that Christ will give me the grace to tell them and them the grace to understand.

Tiffany is already so mature for her age. She is ten going on 16. She had just gotten braces on her teeth and is so cute. She is going through that awkward age when one part of her body seems to outgrow the other parts from time to time. But she has already given her life to Christ for full time Christian service. When she came to tell me that she felt the Lord was calling her to the Mission Field I couldn't hold back the tears. "What's wrong," she asked. Aren't you glad?" "Of course, I'm glad that God has chosen you and I gave you to Him even before you were born. But believe me it was a lot easier THEN than it is NOW sitting here with you." "Then, I just won't go, I'll stay home with you."

"Oh, no Honey, neither of us would be happy if you don't do what the Lord wants you to do. He will give us both the grace when the time comes. We don't have it now, because we don't need it now."

She gave me a big hug and yelled back as she ran out the door – "I love you Mommy."

Not long after this incident Trey told us during our Family Devotions one night that he had felt God was calling him to be a Missionary too. He added that he also wanted to be a pilot. Trey has always wanted to be a pilot for as long as I can remember and I was really shocked when he announced that he felt God wanted him to go into Christian service. "Is there any such thing as a Missionary Pilot"?" "Yes," his Daddy told him, "remember the man who flies supplies over to Haiti and carries the doctors from place to place? He is a missionary." "Then that's what I want to be when I grow up." Of course, I don't know if God is truly preparing them for the Mission Field. I would be lying if I didn't say that I would rather they teach in a Christian school or pastor a church here at home, but I can honestly say that I am WILLING to encourage them in whatever it is God calls them for.

Jeni, our baby is four years old now, and last week invited Christ to come into her heart. She seemed so young that I was amazed when she suggested it, but nevertheless I prayed with her to receive Christ. After she had prayed in her childlike way, she looked up at me with her big, blue eyes and said, " Now if I die, I'll go to Heaven to be with Jesus."

Our family is so busy. The children have piano lessons, gymnastic lessons, horseback riding lessons and homework and on and on. Sometimes I feel like an errand boy taking them here and there and picking up things for O.J. But I can at last say that God has given me the peace and happiness that I never thought I would discover. We have all learned that the secret is to live and love every single minute, not for our own selves only, but for others. That is the secret of true happiness.

Sometimes I am so overcome with wonder that God could love me so much and be so very good to me. O.J. is truly the Prince Charming that I had always dreamed and even more handsome than when we were married 15 years ago. Our marriage has a spark in it that I never dreamed possible. We both find ourselves being silly and romantic like a couple of kids. I had always thought that we had so little in common. Now I find we frequently are thinking the same thoughts. It is almost uncanny, but I will begin to tell O.J. something and he will tell me that he was just about to tell me the same thing.

I remember one incident particularly. I had gone to visit my Mother in Mobile, Alabama for a few days and O.J. was home studying for flight school. Mother told me to buy some material and she would make me a new long skirt. I found this adorable red, white and blue striped fabric that I knew O.J. would love. Mother put the finishing touches on it the day before I was to fly back to Atlanta. I decided to surprise O.J. on Sunday morning with my new outfit so I didn't say anything to him about it before that morning. As I walked out of the bedroom to surprise him, we both were met with a bigger surprise than I could have possibly imagined! O.J. was standing in the hall adjusting his new tie and sporting a brand new sport coat made out of the same EXACT material as my new skirt. As we recounted the days, we had both purchased our new clothes on the very same day. I can't explain it, and won't even begin to try, but I believe that is one of the things the Lord means when he says that " the two shall be one."

On my birthday last year O.J. gave me a new Bible and wrote these words in the front of it. "The words of Solomon 4:1-15 speak better than I ever could about how I think of you. With all my love O.J."

Of course, we know what that says and frankly I am a little embarrassed to write it myself, but God says it is great. (So do I)

Solomon 4:1-15 "Behold, thou art fair, my love: behold, thou art fair; thou hast doves' eyes within thy locks; thy hair is as a flock of goats, that appear from Mount Gilead.

Thy teeth are like a flock of sheep that are even shorn, which came up from the washing whereof every one bear twins, and none is barren among them. Thy lips are like a thread of scarlet, and thy speech is comely; thy temples are like a piece of pomegranate within thy locks. Thy neck is like the tower of David built for an armory, whereon there hang a thousand bucklers. All shields of might men. Thy two breasts are like two young roes that are twins, which feed among the lilies. Until the day break, and the shadows flee away, I will get me to the mountain of myrrh, and to the hill of frankincense.

Thou art all fair, my love, there is no spot in thee. Come with me from Lebanon my spouse, with me from Lebanon; look from the top of Amana, from the top of Shenir and Hermon, from the lion's dens from the mountains of the leopards.

Thou hast ravished my heart, my sister, my spouse, thou has ravished my heart with one of thine eyes, with one chain of thy neck.

How fair is thy love, my sister, my spouse! How much better is thy love than wine! And the smell of thine ointments than all spices!

Thy lips, O my spouse, drop as the honeycomb; honey and milk are under thy tongue; and the smell of thy garments is like the smell of Lebanon.

A garden enclosed is my sister, my spouse; a spring shut up a fountain sealed.

Thy plants are an orchard of pomegranates, with pleasant fruits; camphire, with spikenard.

Spikenard and saffron; calamus and cinnamon, with all trees of frankincense; myrrh and aloes, with all the chief spices;

A fountain of gardens, a well of living water, and streams from Lebanon.[11]

CHAPTER XXV
FLIES, MOSQUITOES AND ME

II Corinthians 12:9 "And He said unto Me, my grace is sufficient for thee…"

There I was at last on the Mission Field! Those two words had intrigued me since I was sixteen years old and I had yearned to see for myself what the Mission Field was like. Now here I was, stepping off an airplane onto the Island of Haiti. "I can't believe I'm really here," I kept thinking to myself.

O.J. and the kids had flown over with me to visit Lee and Barb and see what kind of life Missionaries had on the Island. O.J. planned to help with the building of a hospital in the Mountains where there was not any medical help for miles. As we walked up to the gate at the airport there were lines where people coming into the country were to check in. We found the line that had a sign overhead saying "Visitors Only". It was fascinating to hear the conversations of the people as they waited.

There was a group of young people wearing long dresses and work boots. I was intrigued to learn what they were doing in Haiti. Before long I could hear them talking about the orphanage they were going to build in the mountains. They were so excited that I could almost feel them "bursting at the seams" to get busy. Tiffany was wide eyed! She had never been out of the United States and all the languages were captivating to her. Trey and Jeni stayed close to us and smiled whenever anyone would speak to them.

When we at last made our way to the desk the man spoke in Haitian saying, "Do you have passports?" He could see that we were at a loss for communication, so he spoke in broken English, "Do you have passports?"

Lee had told us that all we needed to get in the country was some type of Identification so we showed him our drivers license. "What about them?" he asked pointing to the children. Not until that moment had I remembered Lee telling me to bring their birth certificates! "O.J.'s going to kill me if they don't let us in," I thought. I had been so excited about the trip that, as usual, I had forgotten half the things I had intended to bring.

"Can't you tell just by looking at them that they are our children?" "No. I.D. no enter country," the man replied. By this time the children were looking a bit like they thought we might leave them there, and I was beginning to think that O.J. might leave us ALL there and go on ahead. But, just then, we saw Lee's blonde head appear in the crowd and O.J. told the man that we were friends of the Baugh's. That seemed to be the magic word and he told us to go on ahead this time, but to bring identification next time. We promised we would and ran off to get our bags from customs.

Lee told us later that this was the same official that helped him when the pilot for West Indies Mission had been killed bringing supplies for the hospital. Haiti had no hospital, so Lee and a group of others had been building one up in the mountains for the past two years. This was where we would be spending much of our time while we were in Haiti.

It was extremely hot and I soon learned that there are no air conditioners in Haiti, only open windows, flies and mosquitoes. "Boy, I'm sure glad to see you guys", Lee told us. "Come, I have the land rover waiting". I found out that cars in Haiti are not air conditioned either. In fact, there are few cars there and we were fortunate to have a ride at all. Most of the people have to ride a little truck with some wooden benches on the back, which they call a "Top Top".

Barb had written and told us about the beautiful house and swimming pool that they were renting while Lee was attending language school. I don't know exactly what I was expecting, but it was not at all the way I had pictured it. As we turned onto the road that led up to the house we had to blow the car horn for the goats to move off the road, and as we approached the house I couldn't see the front door for little black faces. All the Haitian kids had come out to see the new visitors. They were hoping for pennies.

Barb and the three boys were waiting just inside the house for us. We all had a great time hugging and sharing first impressions of the Island. Robby, the eldest had grown so much that I had to look up to talk to him, and Matt who is Trey's age had to show us the baby bird he had caught in the brush. Benjy, the baby wasn't sure what was going on. It was so good to see them again and to see where they were living. Now they wouldn't seem so far away when we prayed for them.

The swimming pool that the kids couldn't wait to jump into turned out to be a big cement hole in the ground, that we had to keep changing the water in to keep it clean. There was no filtration system. But when the temperature became unbearable that water hole was terrific!

We ate most of our meals outside on the patio. As we sat eating, we could see the little Haitian huts about 5ft x 5 ft and the little hungry children running around with no pants on and bellies bulging from starvation. Barb told me that the day before we arrived, a little girl had dropped dead outside her bedroom window, from who knows what. The children just become sick suddenly and die. There are few doctors and no money anyway. As we sat in the living room, the entire house was open. We would watch a bird or large butterfly come in the front door and fly around until it decided to fly out the back door. We were all amazed and just sat and watched all the new happenings with open bewilderment.

The nights were the worst of all. There was no hot water, therefore cold showers were the only way to wash off the sweat and dust. The kids would shake and their lips would chatter, but it was quite an adventure. Then when we would lay down for the night it was so hot that it was impossible to sleep.

The first night we were there as I lay in my bunk thinking over the day's activities, I could hear what sounded like drums in the distance. They gave me a weird feeling, but I finally drifted off to sleep.

"What were those drums we heard last night?" I asked Barb at breakfast. "Oh, those were Voodoo drums. They have ceremonies every night," she told me matter of factly. "Don't they bother you?" I questioned. "No, we plead the Blood of Christ over us and the children and trust Him to take care of us." "They still sacrifice chickens, pigs, and cows to their demon Gods, but we are leading more and more to Christ each day," Lee told us.

As we shopped in the Iron Market the next day, I was careful not to buy anything that had the symbol of Voodoo carved on it. We were the only white people in town and all the merchants thought I was a Missionary since Barbara was. They kept calling us "Mrs. Pastor." It made me very proud, but secretly in my heart I told the Lord, "Thank you that I am not a Missionary. I know now that I am just where You want me."

I'm so thankful for Lee and Barb and all the other people who have left home to come to this place and other places like this to bring the gospel, but at long last I'm so very thankful that I have MY place to bring the gospel, and most of all I'm thankful that it is in Lilburn, Georgia! That was quite an accomplishment for me. I had been repeating those words with my lips for six years, but I believe it was the first time I ever really said them with my heart.

Barb had finished her language school and was preparing to move inland to the mountains where they were building the hospital. It was decided that the men would drive the land rover and take the older children, and Barb and I would fly over with the two babies. I thought we were getting off easy, since it was a six hour trip by car. But when we arrived at the airport and went to the Aire Haiti gate, I couldn't find the airplane! "It's that one over there", Barb said pointing to a small two engine, six seater plane. "You mean THAT one!" I have never been too fond of flying and the prospects of getting on that little plane scared me out of my wits. Finally, she convinced me that if I wanted to see the hospital, this was the only way....All Aboard! Jeni kept wanting to know when they would put out the seat belt lights so that we could walk around and I just kept praying I would be able to walk again, SOMEDAY!! We had to hold the kids on our laps and we all were miserably crowded. Clouds was all I could see until at long last we started down...I could see land!

The mountains were all around and I kept wondering where the airport was. Barb told me not to be nervous if the pilot had to go around the landing strip a couple of times, because he usually had to buzz it to get the cows off. Still I don't believe I was prepared for what my eyes saw! We were landing in the middle of a CORN FIELD! That was the runway??!!

Finally, I saw a little shack about the size of my kitchen at home, unpainted and tilting to one side. "That's it", I was told. As we landed six old men came walking slowly out to get our luggage. They were chewing tobacco and were so thin that I didn't see how they could pick up those heavy suitcases. The kids were fascinated and I was in shock! No one (O.J. and Lee) was there to meet us and it was another two hours ride up the mountains to the hospital. I was really beginning to think I should have stayed in town.

Barb sent a note to some other Missionaries in the nearby town to please come pick us up. One thing I learned that day, NO ONE in Haiti hurries! Finally, our driver did come and was smiling from ear to ear. It was only the sixth month he had been driving. Before that time he had never seen a hammer or anything mechanical. Now our lives were to be entrusted to this "smiling nut" as he drove around those steep curves atop the mountains, swaying from one side to the other. "What in the world am I doing here?" I asked myself. As we drove along the bumpy dirt road we passed the man carrying the note Barb had sent to her friends. "Thank the Lord we didn't have to wait for them to come get us."

"We have to stop and pick up supplies", the driver told us. "Oh, no", I thought. It was near lunch time and I knew the kids were hungry, but I knew I shouldn't cause any trouble, so I said nothing. The stop was at a medical clinic and Barb knew all the nurses. They were very gracious and fed us lunch. (I still wonder what it was.)

The sights along the road were beautiful and pitiful at the same time. The water from the ocean would come right up to the road at places and look like one of those inviting tropical Island advertisements, but closer observation would always show a few hungry kids standing in the waves hoping for a fish or any other thing they might pick up. I was beginning to think we would never reach "Hospital Lumiere", which means Hospital of Light, but at long last we did.

We had run out of road about an hour ago and could see nothing but rocks and hills and a few trees, until finally as we topped one hill, Jill, the driver shouted, "There it is"! I could see the love he had for the hospital and what it meant to his people from the look on his face. The Haitians are truly humble and grateful people. They knew the sacrifices that the Baughs and others were making for them.

O.J. and Lee still were not there and I began to worry. I could imagine all the treacherous places where they might have wrecked. As we walked into the house where Lee and Barb would be making their home, I was speechless. It was gray concrete block, with gray concrete floors. There were no screens on the windows and no electricity! Barb was so proud to be at their final destination after many long years of waiting. "We're home," she told Benjy. I couldn't hold back my tears as I thought about my own home and how I would complain if my carpets were soiled. Why, I couldn't bear it when my dishwasher went on the blink last month. Now, there were our very dear friends, grateful just to be where the Lord wanted them.

In the distance we could hear the roar of the motor from the land rover. They had made it! My heart raced to think of all the stories the children would have to tell from their trip across Haiti in that bouncing jeep!

Their faces were all lit up, no worse for the wear. (But they were so hyper after sitting and bouncing all those hours that we had a hard time quieting them down.) They had run out of road just as we had and crossing the rivers was a real life adventure for them. Trey especially loved it!! It was like camping out for him.

As Matt walked into his room we could hear yells and stomping from him and Trey. "Mommy, there's a big spider in my room." It was a huge black tarantula! I had chills all up and down my back. I could envision sleeping here tonight and with no lights, and being visited by his mate.

"It'll be nice when we get it painted and some curtains, don't you think"? Barb was asking me. "Nice!" I thought, "yes nice that it's you and not me!" But their sweet attitude and love for the people there showed me that THEY were glad it was them too. I felt ashamed for my bad attitudes and fears.

Fred Brown was the surgeon there and the only doctor at the hospital. He offered for O.J. to make rounds with them that afternoon and off they went. When O.J. came back to the house, he had a different understanding of the work that they were doing on that mountain. He described to me in vivid detail, as only a pilot can do, just what was wrong with all the people they visited. One of them was a little boy suffering from tuberculosis. They had drained his lungs and gotten a gallon of fluid. He was very sick, but was going to live, and as a result of being brought to the hospital, had found Christ.

I cautioned the children to stay away from inside the hospital, but Trey found it irresistible. He and Matt would ride their bikes around and around the grounds. At dinner that night Fred told us that he had to run the boys out of the operating room that afternoon. He had been working on the boy with tuberculosis and Trey, Matt, and Robby came wondering in to see what was going on. I couldn't believe my ears!

Now I supposed Trey would get tuberculosis! I knew it was very contagious!! That was about all I could handle. I wanted to beat him and scream at him, but I knew it was best to let his Daddy take care of this incident. O.J. explained to Trey how dangerous it was for him to go into that operating room, not only for him, but for that pitiful boy that was so sick. They could have contaminated him with germs that would have killed him. All the boys were truly sorry when they realized how careless they had been.

Sunday morning we all dressed up and walked down the rocky path to church. It was in a small unpainted shack no larger than my living room. The pastor was Haitian. The ushers were Haitian, so were all the songs. I couldn't understand anything that they said, could only hum when they sang the hymns, but I felt the presence of the Lord in that little group of strangers who had been converted from Voodoo to my Lord and Savior, Jesus Christ. It was a wonderful experience, to see them singing praises to the true God where they had once been chanting songs to their demon gods.

It was Friday before we knew it and time to leave for the airport to go back home. We had loved the Baughs for many years, and now we had made other friends at the hospital that we hated to leave. Fred and Hannie Brown had instantly become good friends. It was as if we had known them all our lives and now we had to leave them. Being on that Missionary Compound had been like a little bit of Heaven with only Christians around and we hated to leave that atmosphere. We hugged everybody's necks and positioned ourselves in the land rover. Even the children cried and hated to say good-bye. As we came to the bottom of the mountain we could see them all waving to us from the top of the Brown's house.

No one talked much on the trip back. We were all so tired and sad to be leaving. We were hoping to get a flight back home the next morning since O.J. was scheduled to go back to work on Monday. We raced to the plane with our arms full of trinkets and souvenirs we had bought on the Island. There weren't enough seats for all of us to sit together, so the children sat in front of us. It was good to be cool again in that air conditioned airplane and we all sat silently just enjoying the quiet. My mind was racing with all the memories I had collected and all the lessons that the Lord had taught me in Haiti. I had a grateful spirit that I prayed I would never loose. I believe the children were thinking some of the same thoughts.

Suddenly, Tiffany leaned over and whispered to me, "Mommy, my ear hurts. Do you think it could be infected?" I felt her, and sure enough she had a fever. We would have to stop by the doctor's office as soon as we landed.

"Mommy, I can't find my wooden donkey that Benjy gave me," Jeni began to cry.

"I need to go to the rest room!" Trey announced to the entire plane load of people.

"Oh, HELP!" I thought.

Just then O.J. turned and smiled at me. We both knew a wonderful secret. Our desperate search was over. The happiness for which we had longed was right here with us, right in our own hearts! We didn't have to go anywhere else to live, or to serve, not even on the Mission Field. We didn't have to buy anything, or look any further. At long last we discovered God's will for us, our family. I could hardly wait to get back home to share all these things.

I wish I could end by saying, "And they lived happily ever after." Of course, I can't! We still have problems, the kids still get sick, and sometimes we get discouraged. But one thing is always true – the view from this side, The Happy Side, is breath-taking!

Would you like to see your manuscript become a book?

If you are interested in becoming a PublishAmerica author, please submit your manuscript for possible publication to us at:

acquisitions@publishamerica.com

You may also mail in your manuscript to:

**PublishAmerica
PO Box 151
Frederick, MD 21705**

www.publishamerica.com

CPSIA information can be obtained at www.ICGtesting.com
Printed in the USA
240026LV00001B/82/P